ELVIS PEOPLE

Ted Harrison is a former BBC Religious Affairs Correspondent. His is a regular voice on BBC Radio 4 and he is also a presenter of the ITV Series The Human Factor. His study of the Elvis cult is his ninth book, and he has previously written about, amongst others, Catherine Bramwell Booth, the athlete Kriss Akabusi and David Jenkins, Bishop of Durham.

Ted Harrison

ELVIS PEOPLE

☆ ☆ ☆

The Cult of the King

Fount
An Imprint of HarperCollinsPublishers

Fount Paperbacks is an Imprint of
HarperCollins*Religious*
Part of HarperCollins*Publishers*
77–85 Fulham Palace Road, London W6 8JB

First published in Great Britain
in 1992 by Fount Paperbacks

3 5 7 9 10 8 6 4 2

A catalogue record for this book is
available from the British Library

ISBN 0 00 627620 2

Typeset by Avocet Typesetters, Bicester, Oxon
Printed and bound in Great Britain by
HarperCollinsManufacturing, Glasgow

Contents

Acknowledgements

My thanks go to all the Elvis fans who spoke to me freely and honestly: to Sid Shaw and Todd Slaughter of the two British fan clubs, in particular *Elvisly Yours* for permission to quote from the club magazine.

I had much help from John Newbury when we visited Memphis gathering Elvis material for BBC radio and for me to research the book. I would also like to thank the Christian ministers from Memphis who shared their thoughts. I am also grateful to Harold Loyd and the staff at Graceland. And finally I would like to thank the many people whose writings I have studied and sometimes quoted in the course of the book.

INTRODUCTION

☆

The Elvis Cult

Many attempts have been made to understand the great Elvis Presley phenomenon. No other entertainer has ever held such a grip on the imagination of millions of people around the world. His fans do not bother to compare his success with that of other pop stars or entertainers. He is in a league of his own.

Not even The Beatles or Marilyn Monroe have invaded the psyche and culture of so many people. Over and over again his followers claim Elvis was the greatest man to walk this earth since Jesus Christ.

Elvis is not just a pop phenomenon, or even a social one. Elvis, either the myth or the man, touches something deeper. Perhaps he reaches through to the eternal spirit in all of us, which yearns for truth, meaning and purpose in a cruel, incomprehensible and uncomprehending world. The worship, adoration and the perpetuation of the memory of Elvis today, closely resembles a religious cult. Indeed, what is now the Elvis cult could be nothing less than a religion in embryo. A cult is a temporary phenomenon in which spiritual ideas are focused sharply on the life, leadership or teaching of an individual. A cult grows into a religion the longer it survives and the more the followers of the founding figure make claims that they have discovered a unique truth inspired by God.

In the beginning there was the word, and the word was Elvis.

This quote, attributed to one of America's leading Elvis impersonators, is a grotesque parody of the opening words of St John's gospel. Yet thousands of Elvis fans willingly endorse the sentiments expressed, and they themselves would be shocked to think that by making that endorsement, they too could stand accused of blasphemous bad taste. It is one measure of how far the admiration of a twentieth-century entertainer has turned into a new religious movement.

It is fifteen years since Elvis Presley's death was reported. Today his home, Graceland, in Memphis, Tennessee, is a focus of pilgrimage. The simple two-roomed wooden shack in Tupelo, Mississippi, where he was born, is preserved as a shrine. Nearby is a chapel dedicated to the memory of Elvis.

Elvis is constantly referred to as "The King". His life story is told and retold by the fans, in a legendary form, which takes the shape of a gospel. Devotees buy icons and relics of Elvis and write messages to him, declarations of love which are frequently couched in religious language. They see Elvis as having had Messianic qualities and a divine destiny. Fans pray to, or through, Elvis and describe him as a bridge between themselves and God. His archive of recorded music has, to many fans, the authority of scripture. Their copies of his records are kept apart from other records; they are reverenced and frequently consulted for inspiration and guidance. There is an Elvis priesthood, the impersonators who are seen to represent the body of Elvis to his people here on earth. Elvis fans collect for charity and do good works in his name. They claim for Elvis the power of healing. Some talk of feeling his presence. Others even say they have seen him in his resurrected form.

So it is that watching the cult of Elvis Presley develop could provide scholars with many fascinating insights into the way other faiths have taken shape in their early days.

The first few years after someone, who is seen as a prophet or inspired religious leader, leaves his followers behind, are crucial. For in those years, while the generation who knew the leader first hand are still living, the religion takes shape. It is the time when myths about the prophet turn into the "facts"

10

about his life and message. These become "facts" which future adherents can never dispute. This is what could now be happening in the case of Elvis. And if a resurrection story can grow up around a pop singer, and be believed by his fans, how can Christians be sure that the same psychological mechanism was not at work amongst the early Christians?

Over the centuries many cults and religions have been started. The Elvis cult is one of the latest. There have been emperors who have been worshipped, saints, gurus, charlatans and even pets who have been the focus of devotion. Each cult has been a product of its time and nurturing society. Most have petered out after a few years. Only time will tell if the Elvis shrines will still be decorated and lovingly tended, two hundred, let alone two thousand, years from now. Much will depend on the survival of the Elvis myth, particularly the spiritual elements associated with it. For the music and writings of many of the great artists of the past have survived the test of time, but the commemorations of these artists themselves have not formed the basis of cults. Cults and new religions only form around a prophet or personality whose projected image and sustaining aura feeds a spiritual hunger. These people are said to have charisma, in the literal sense, a gift from God.

*

It is not necessary to visit Graceland to see examples of the way the followers of Elvis celebrate and remember their hero. Every year, for instance, a group of British fans gather at a holiday camp at Hemsby in Norfolk.

There gather the young, for whom Elvis Presley has always been a hero from the past. There are the middle-aged, men and women, who had known of Elvis first when he was their teenage idol. There are the older fans, converts to the Presley sound later in life.

At the climax of the Elvis Festival, the compere takes the stage in the ballroom.

"Give me an 'E'," he shouts to the thousand strong crowd.

" 'E' ", they roar in response.

"Give me an 'L', give me a 'V', give me an 'I', give me an 'S'." With each letter the response grows louder.

"Who's going to live for ever?"

"ELVIS!"

And then the chant begins, "Elvis, Elvis, Elvis, Elvis. . . ." Many in the audience sway as they chant and hold their hands in the air as if they were at a pentecostal service. They call out to Elvis as Christians at an evangelical rally might call out the name of Jesus. In fact the compere's routine, "E-L-V-I-S, Who's going to live for ever?" is a direct copy of a Christian rallying call, only Elvis's name is substituted for that of Jesus.

Yet Elvis fans insist they mean no disrespect to Jesus. Elvis, they say, was a devout Christian himself. His greatest music, many say, was his gospel music. Nevertheless, they persistently borrow the language of Christianity in order to express their devotion to Elvis. Perhaps this is because it is the only spiritual language they have to hand. What is significant is that the fans feel the need to use spiritual terms, allegories and liturgies to express their feelings of devotion. For Elvis, to them, is more than a mortal hero. He was, in the view of thousands of devotees, the greatest man to walk the earth since Jesus. Some look to Elvis's own study of New Age ideas and esoteric writings for evidence that he was sent to earth to fulfil a great spiritual mission; a mission perhaps with a particular apocalyptic relevance. Many fans also talk of their personal relationship with him, and speak in terms very close to those used by many Christians to describe their personal relationship with Jesus.

As the years go by there seems to be no diminution in the interest in Elvis. People who could never have known him as part of their youth experience, and could therefore have no nostalgic yearning for their "King", now profess themselves to be fans. Residents of Memphis talk of growing numbers arriving each year to take part in the annual Elvis week at Graceland.

Attempts are sometimes made to explain this continuing and increasing interest in Elvis Presley in secular or cultural terms.

Some see it simply as a temporary American social aberration. Yet, although much of it is rooted in a specific view of the world which has its origins in the southern states of the USA, it has a wider appeal. As with Christianity, word of the Messiah has spread to the Gentiles. In Britain and historic western Europe, where much which comes out of the brash new culture evolving on the other side of the Atlantic Ocean is dismissed with a certain contempt as being modern, vulgar and tacky, Elvis followers can be numbered in their thousands. The message has even penetrated what was the USSR. In the days of the communists, Elvis fans met in secret to talk of the "King" and play his music. If caught by the authorities, it is said, fans were arrested and persecuted for their deviance from the acceptable political code.

The suggestion has been made that Elvis's popularity can be explained in these terms, that he symbolized the ultimate rebellion of all ordinary folk against all forms of restraint. Yet this is a very limited explanation. Elvis was only a true rebel at the beginning of his career. By the time his death was reported he was to his public the model American. John Lennon said of his one-time idol, "Elvis died the day he went into the army".

The only way, it would seem, to explain truly the Elvis phenomenon and understand the movement, is to see it in spiritual terms. It is a cult, maybe a religion in the making, which has already gathered to itself the trappings of a faith.

ONE

☆

The Elvis Gospel

Theologians have argued for centuries over the details of faith; similarly, students of Elvis Presley debate the details of the life of their hero. What matters to both groups is not so much what can be proved to be literally true, in all such debates literal and undisputable truth is hard to come by, but what is believed to be true. The Elvis story, as with all legends, is made up of that blend of myth and fact which, when combined, stimulate powerful emotions in the mind of a devotee.

As with the New Testament account of the birth of Christ, the story of Elvis starts with the legend of his conception. At the very moment that Elvis was conceived his father, Vernon, it is said, lost consciousness. A sign, Elvis came to believe later, that his father was used at that moment for a higher purpose, as the vehicle or conduit of a higher being. Vernon was thus father to Elvis in the same way that Joseph was father to Jesus. The story confirmed in Elvis's mind during his studies of mysticism and the occult that he, Elvis Aron Presley, might be a Master or Messenger from God sent to earth for some great purpose.

The Australian rock 'n' roll singer Nick Cave is not a typical Elvis fan, but his Album *The Firstborn is Dead* is one of the most powerful, mystical tellings of the Elvis story. He dispenses with any run of the mill interpretation of Elvis Presley's birth, and gives it mystical qualities.

And the black rain came down,
Water water everywhere.
Where no bird can fly no fish can swim.
No fish can swim until the King is born!
Until the King is born! In Tupelo! Tupelo! Til the King is
   born in Tupelo!

Tupelo, where Elvis Presley was born in poverty and obscurity,
was then a small and insignificant Mississippi town. The most
important event in the town's history took place on 8 January,
1935. The exact place of Elvis's birth was the front room of
a tiny two-roomed wooden shack of a house, little bigger than
a stable. It was a night both of joy and tragedy, for Elvis was
one of identical twins born to Gladys Love Presley. His brother
was stillborn, and buried later in an unmarked grave. The twin
was named Jesse Garon. Gladys was sure the twins were
identical and thus Elvis came from "the root of Jesse". Reading
religious significance into coincidences and word-play is popular
amongst Elvis fans. To have come from the root of Jesse is
a direct reference to the biblical genealogy of Jesus, which traces
him back to King David and his father Jesse. Later Elvis came
to accept that he had part Jewish ancestry, yet was reluctant
to talk about it.

A strange story about the night of the double birth was told
by Elvis's father, Vernon, that with the wind blowing outside,
a mysterious blue light appeared over and around the place
where Elvis lay as a newborn baby struggling for life.

Nick Cave's song summons up a mystery from the mundane
grief, fear, panic and triumph of the moment.

Well, Saturday gives what Sunday steals.
And a child is born on his brother's heels,
Come Sunday morn the firstborn is dead,
In a shoe-box tied with a ribbon of red. Tupelo! Hey Tupelo!
In a shoe-box tied with a ribbon of red!

Some people claim the name Elvis was a family one and could

be of Viking origin meaning "all wise". Others argue the origins of the first syllable, "El", can be found, not in a Nordic past, but in references to God made in a number of faiths, as in Bethel, the hallowed spot or House of God. Whatever its significance it cannot be denied that the name is an anagram of Lives, a fact which the fans who indulge in word-play are keen to point out. Aron is biblical in origin, with Aaron being the brother of Moses. The name is given three possible meanings: teacher, singer or messenger. What all three words have in common is the notion of communicator. Presley has been said by fans to be a surname corrupted from the word "Priestly".

All these attempts to give special interpretations to the name have occurred since Elvis became famous. Some New Testament scholars might argue they are similar to the attempts made by the gospel writers to write the story of Jesus in such a way that it could be seen to tie in with the Old Testament prophecies. There is nothing dishonest in this. If a person is convinced the story being told is of universal significance, then it is inevitable that, with hindsight, the details of the story are also seen to have great meaning.

A whimsical account of the boyhood of Elvis is given in a book called *The Illustrated Elvis*, by W.A. Harbinson, published in New York two years before Elvis's death. Under a family snapshot of Elvis, aged six, posed with his parents, the writer describes the boy in the picture.

Dressed in local style, with a long-sleeved white shirt, open at the neck, and ragged trousers tugged chest-high by braces: he is Huckleberry Finn.

The great myths of America lie behind him. Born of a family that is scourged by its own poverty, maybe he already dreams some heady dreams. In this land that he roams, through the cotton fields and swamplands, the air is heavy with the romance of its own history. The Union and Confederate armies have clashed on these slopes, the town has been razed in the fury of civil strife, and the Indians have left names that will roll on the tongue with all the magic of ancient hieroglyphics: this land is a dreamer's masque.

The boy will sense this if he doesn't quite realize it. He will learn to love God, to respect even his worst elders, and to stand by country right or wrong. He wanders through the bellied fields . . . puts his ear to the wind and listens closely. The air is filled with singing that came out of slave ships, now pours from black lips, fills white churches. It is the singing of the blacks who have given to the white man a culture he will never acknowledge: it is American Gospel.

The writer continues to talk of the merging of black and white culture in the churches. The congregations might remain segregated but their style of worship and feel for music are shared. "The singing comes as naturally as breathing: it is part of his heritage. He lives in the very seat of American folk music . . . White music is hillbilly, black music is the blues, and some day the two will have to meet."

There will be many people today who will argue that Elvis's greatest contribution to music was one that he himself was probably unaware of, but which stems from this time: that he introduced the riches of black music to a white audience. In the course of just one generation, pop music became not only totally multi-racial, but in many areas the main innovations were inspired by black performers. Elvis brought a sensuality to popular music, best illustrated by the way he moved his own body to his music. To quote from Samuel Roy's book, *Elvis, Prophet of Power*, "Elvis's singing was an emancipation; his movements were a revelation". Many of the older generation were scandalized. The way they saw Elvis using his body challenged and disturbed suppressed sexual feelings. He also brought racial prejudices to the surface. What was this nice white boy doing pretending to be a nigger? White Southern society of the fifties was oppressive both of the black population and of its own inner feelings. Elvis threatened it with a double emancipation.

18

The story of the boyhood of Elvis tends now to be told in episodes. And each episode has its own meaning, usually one which points to one of the talents or qualities Elvis was later to display as an adult.

One Christmas, so goes a story told by the Presley family, young Elvis badly wanted a tricycle as a present. His parents saved hard and bought him one. Gladys would do anything to indulge her only surviving son. When Christmas Day dawned, Elvis had the present he wanted. He took it out for his first ride, but returned a little later to the house without it. His mother asked what had happened to it. Elvis said he had given it away to a little boy who had not had any presents for Christmas. His mother, who had saved so hard to get the tricycle, went and got it back, but Elvis promptly gave it away again.

Elvis's talent was first discovered while in the fifth grade at Lawhon Elementary School. He was at the time a shy and quirky ten-year-old child who was adored by, and had an unusually close relationship with, his mother. Indeed throughout their life together Elvis and Gladys talked to each other using an exclusive baby-talk between themselves. But when he was asked to sing in front of his class, the image changed. He gave no half-hearted rendition. His talent was such that he was entered for a local talent contest and won second prize. He sang the maudlin ballad, *Old Shep*, which tells the story of the death of a loyal dog.

Being the only child, Elvis spent much time amusing himself. He often became absorbed in the comic books of the time, identifying with the characters. In her biography of Gladys Presley, Elaine Dundy tells a story, which may help understand the course Elvis took later in life when he began searching for an explanation for his life and success.

Elvis read the Captain Marvel story *Atlantis Rises Again*, set in the thirteenth-thousandth century, in which the secret of Captain Marvel Jr's super-human powers are revealed.

Marvel Jr, the most powerful boy in the world, is asked his name by Chass, another character in the story.

Marvel Jr begins, "Why, I'm Captain Mar . . . er . . . uh . . ." And then he halts. Why?

On the last panel on the page is the explanation: "Captain Marvel Jr, alone of the Marvel family, always has a peculiar problem when people ask his name for . . ." And then Marvel Jr explains it to his readers in a thought balloon: it seems that whenever he tells his name the magic lightning comes and those words, Captain Marvel, make him change back into poor Freddy Freeman! So he hesitates. However, as he is so far in the future, he decides: why not disclose his true powerful identity? What has he to lose?

"I'm Captain Marvel Jr of the twentieth century," he says.

Boom! More lightning zig-zags with the uttering of the two key words. For with the telling of his name, he is transformed back into Freddy Freeman, the poor crippled newsboy.

Thirteenth-thousandth century Chass is astonished. "What. . . . What! There are two of you."

"Yes," says Freddy, "you see we change back and forth by magic lightning. It's safe to tell you because this is far from the twentieth century! Nobody knows my secret back there."

In short, Elvis must constantly be on guard against declaring himself to anyone, for if his outrageous secret were known he would no longer be the Most Powerful Boy in the World."

Later in life, when he began his course of esoteric reading and study, his outrageous boyhood fantasies took new shape. He began to share them with others who, in turn, encouraged him and even suggested the fantasies might have some basis in fact. He also adopted the Captain Marvel bolt of lightning as his personal motif.

In 1946, on Elvis's eleventh birthday, Gladys bought her son his first guitar from the hardware store in Tupelo. The story goes that Elvis asked for a gun for his birthday, but his mother would not buy him one and only reluctantly did he accept a substitute.

In the summer of 1948 Vernon and Gladys Presley had to flee from Tupelo to find shelter in the city of Memphis across the state border in Tennessee. Possibly the family was in danger from creditors; certainly it was under continual threat from the grinding poverty of the age. Vernon was not popular with the Tupelo authorities, having already served a gaol sentence for forgery. One story has it that Vernon was given two weeks to leave town. A hint here of a parallel with the child Jesus' flight into Egypt to escape the dangers of his homeland.

The Presley family did not succeed in escaping from poverty. Vernon moved from job to job, and the family lived in the poorest part of town. By now Elvis was growing up and his distinctive personality was developing. Shy and a loner, he was at the same time distinctive with his sideburns and greasy hair. In down-town Memphis Elvis heard the music of the street. He had his guitar and practised regularly. The idea was forming in his mind that he might become a musician. It was a dull time to be young. The music on the radio was tedious and the youth culture was only just beginning to take shape.

At school Elvis did little to distinguish himself, except make certain important friends, notably with Robert "Red" West, who was to join him as one of his companions, the Memphis Mafia, and who would ultimately, so fans say, betray him. His talents as a singer were, however, noticed and he performed in the Humes High School annual minstrel show. He was number sixteen on the programme, described simply as guitarist. He was followed by a tap dancing display.

Towards the end of his time at school Elvis began to take part-time jobs to supplement the family income, and when he finally left school at the age of eighteen he went to work for the Crown Electric Company.

The oft-told tale of how an unpromising Memphis teenager became a world super-star starts in 1953, when Elvis paid a visit to the Memphis Recording Service at Union Avenue. It was a small studio, where any member of the public could pay his or her money and make a demo disc. Elvis wished, so the legend goes, to make a record for his mother. Elvis scholars, more interested in facts, now suggest he deliberately went there hoping the owner, Sam Phillips, would hear him sing.

Sam Phillips, however, was not there, but his secretary was and she recognized in the young Elvis Presley a quality of voice which she felt her boss would like to hear. So she made her own recording of Elvis singing. Later Sam Phillips heard the tape and liked it, although not enough to call Elvis back for an audition.

A few months later, in January 1954, Elvis returned to the studio to pay another four dollars to make a record. He deliberately chose to call midweek and not on a Saturday, so that Sam Phillips would hear him. This time Elvis had his way, but Sam Phillips, although he liked the sound, did not offer an instant contract.

Six months was to pass before Elvis got his chance. It was in June that Sam Phillips was looking for a singer to record a song called *Without You*. His secretary/office manager remembers Elvis. They call him up. He agrees to record the song and is awful. Nothing goes right for Elvis.

"What can you get right?" asks Sam Phillips. Elvis zips through his repertoire. Sam is hooked. He puts Elvis to work to get the style right. Looking for, as Sam Phillips put it, a white boy who could sing like a black man, he thinks he has found him in Elvis.

The first play of his first record on air, on a Memphis radio station, sets the Elvis career moving. *That's All Right Mama*, is an instant success.

For the next three and a half years Elvis became, in the eyes of the older generation, the country's most corrupting influence. His pelvic movements on television, his loud defiant music, his curled lip, half smile-half sneer, seemed to tear at the very fabric of decent society. He exuded sexuality. Young women screamed for him. His life was no longer his own. Elvis was to the youth of America the saviour they were waiting for. The man, the image and the sound to lift them from apathy and boredom.

It is hard now to imagine at a distance of nearly forty years the effect he had. He epitomized rebellion. He was a social danger. He became an instant role model and object of sexual desire. He learned how to play an audience and could whip them to a state of hysteria. He was often in physical danger from the sobbing, screaming, uncontrollable fans. He unleashed the pent-up emotions of a whole generation. And once *Heartbreak Hotel* was released Elvis was also on course to earning fabulous sums of money.

That department of his affairs, however, came to be handed over to a certain Colonel Thomas Parker. He was a phoney colonel and, as it was to be revealed much later, an illegal American immigrant, but he succeeded in getting and keeping control of all Elvis's business matters until Elvis's death. Only then did a court case reveal how he had been helping himself over-lavishly to his protégé's earnings.

The colonel contracted Elvis to make a succession of films, and he had made four, including *Jailhouse Rock* and *Love Me Tender*, when Elvis's life changed abruptly.

On 24 March, 1958, Elvis Presley was drafted into the army. From being the American social *bête noire*, Elvis became the Pentagon press department's greatest asset. But being put into uniform was not to be the biggest blow to Elvis in that one year. In 1958 his mother, Gladys, died at the age of forty-six. Elvis was devastated. Many fans say he was never the same again. Despite the many triumphs and hit records to come, they chart his downfall from the day he lost the comfort and guiding hand of his mother.

Within two years Vernon Presley had remarried (Elvis did not attend the wedding), and Elvis had met the woman he was to marry. Priscilla Beaulieu was a schoolgirl living with her parents in West Germany. A few months after Elvis was discharged from the army in 1960, he telephoned Priscilla's father to ask that his daughter be allowed to come and live at Graceland, the mansion house in Memphis he had bought. The arrangements were made, including those for Priscilla to continue with her school studies.

For most of the nineteen sixties Elvis's career was on hold. While The Beatles and Rolling Stones were touring and capturing the attention of the world, he had been scheduled by the colonel to spend his time on the film set. It provided a regular income for the colonel, but few of the films impressed the critics.

In May 1967 Elvis married Priscilla, and nine months later, on 1 February, 1968, their only child, Lisa Marie, was born. Some cynics even argue that the marriage only took place at the insistence of the colonel, who wanted the publicity to boost Elvis's flagging career. The marriage lasted until 1972, when Priscilla left Elvis for her karate instructor.

What, however, succeeded in giving Elvis a new lease of life was the television show he shot for NBC, which was shown in December 1968. After a decade of inactivity, a mature Elvis appeared resurrected. In her article in *International Folklore Review* in 1984, Sue Bridwell Beckham draws a religious parallel.

At the mythic age of thirty-three, the age at which Jesus was tried, crucified and rose from the dead, Elvis taped a concert in front of a live audience which would be aired via satellite around the world. Thus Elvis arose. The television concert was hailed as a revival and even as a "resurrection". It paved the way for his first public appearance in nearly a decade in Las Vegas, and for continual live concerts at a spirit-breaking pace until his death in 1977. Thus he became again a "living" musical guru who had flesh and blood contact with his followers. But it would take his death to bring about the transfiguration.

It was also around the late sixties, and just before the great revival, that Elvis began to explore certain philosophical ideas and wonder about his calling and purpose. He had come under the influence of Larry Geller, who was employed as a hairdresser, but was much more beside. The stories told of Elvis at this time are of a changed character. The shy schoolkid had long passed into history. So had the rebellious youth who terrified middle America. The exemplary conscript had also given way. What had emerged was a new Elvis, the product of almost a decade of a kind of imprisonment. All that time he had little contact with the real world. His time was spent in Hollywood or Graceland. Because of his status as an illegal immigrant, the colonel dare not ask for a passport to enable him to take Elvis on tour abroad. Elvis had become introspective and out of touch, his mind filled with a whole range of new ideas and possibilities. He had an ecstatic vision one day, travelling through the Arizonan desert, believing he had seen Christ and the Antichrist.

On another occasion when Elvis was listening to a bird singing, he turned to a companion and said that in the sound of the warbling of the bird, he had just heard the voice of Jesus.

He also attempted to practise faith healing, as when Brian, the small son of two of Elvis's close companions, was suffering from a burning fever. Elvis took a green scarf and laid the boy upon it, green being the colour of healing. Elvis then put on a turban decorated with a large stone and sat by the boy, meditating. He touched little Brian on various parts of his body, while the child looked on with fascination at the pop star's exotic head-dress. Elvis commanded the fever to leave the boy and enter Elvis himself. The next day the fever left. "Good," said Elvis, "that pleases me."

Many stories also came to be told of Elvis Presley's private acts of generosity. His first cousin, Harold Loyd, nephew of Gladys Presley, tells of a number he witnessed. In his account of his time working for Elvis as gatekeeper, a book he wrote called *Elvis Presley's Graceland Gates*, he tells of these two instances.

A family that lived on a farm plantation in Arkansas had their home burned down. They lost everything including one of their children. Elvis had his dad buy a used pick-up truck, loaded it with clothes and food (only God knows what else he gave) and took it to them.

Another time he was on his way home (to Graceland),

probably from the movies, when he saw a pick-up truck parked on the side of the street. The truck was loaded with cardboard paper. He asked the driver to stop and got out and went over to the truck. There was a black man and his wife standing there beside the truck. Elvis asked him what the trouble was and he told him the driveshaft was broken. He asked the man how much he thought it would cost to fix it and he told Elvis the amount, adding that he didn't have the money. Elvis took his checkbook and wrote him a check. I never knew (or asked) the amount but he told the man if he had any trouble getting the check cashed, to have the bank call him or his father and they would verify it."

*

And the Elvis legend began to gather to it a supernatural dimension. There was once a thunderstorm over Graceland and a bolt of lightning struck a marble statue in the Meditation Garden. The only damage was a mark left on the statue which resembled the shape of the lightning bolt itself. Elvis believed it to be a sign from God. He adopted the shape, similar too to the lightning strike of Captain Marvel, as the logo for his companions – known by others on the Graceland staff as the Memphis Mafia. They were employed to attend to every Elvis whim, and had to do everything he required in double-quick time, whatever he demanded. They had to Take Care of Business in a flash. So the TCB logo struck through with a lightning bolt came into being. Elvis, it is said, was buried with a TCB diamond ring.

He wore other items of jewellery, each with its significance. Around his neck Elvis wore both a Star of David and the Cross of Jesus.

*

The gospels tell stories of Jesus addressing vast crowds. He must indeed have been a spell-binding performer to have held the attention of a hungry five-thousand-strong audience. We know the gist of what he said, but one can only imagine what it must have been like to have been there. From 1954 to 1977, with the break in the sixties, Elvis gave hundreds of concerts throughout the USA. Yet because his manager had no passport, Elvis was never taken on a world tour. In the final years an Elvis concert could be something of a hit or miss affair. He was often overweight, suffering from the side-effects of his over-prescribed drugs, and only the loyalty of his fans saw him through. In his prime, from all accounts, he was the most electrifying entertainer of all time. He employed all the tricks of stage hype and lighting, wore dazzling clothes, and had the talent of appearing to everyone in the audience as if he were addressing each intimate song directly at him or her individually.

To get a flavour of Elvis at his greatest, it is perhaps best to turn to an account written by someone who is not a dedicated fan. Indeed he is detested by many followers of Elvis for his book about their idol, in which he wrote a "warts and all" portrait of the man so many adore.

This is Albert Goldman's account of Elvis in Las Vegas in 1969, which first appeared in *Life* magazine.

Gorgeous! – or some equally effusive effeminate word – is the only way to describe Elvis Presley's latest epiphany at Las Vegas. Not since Marlene Dietrich stunned the ringsiders with the sight of those legs encased from hip to ankle in a transparent gown has any performer so electrified this jaded town with a personal appearance. Without twanging a string, burbling a note or offering a hint of help, Elvis transfixed a tough opening-night audience of flacks and entertainers simply by striding on-stage in the Costume of the Year.

What was he wearing? Nothing lavish, my dear, just a smashing white jump suit, slashed to the sternum and lovingly fitted around his broad shoulders, flat belly, narrow hips and . . . well, it's a nice fit. And then there are his pearls – loads of lustrous pearls, not sewn on his costume but worn unabashed as body ornaments. Pearls coiled in thick bunches around his neck, pearls girdled his tapered waist in a fabulous karate belt: rope of pearl alternated with rope of gold, the whole sash tied over one hip with the ends brushing his left knee.

With his massive diamonds flashing pinks and purples from his fingers and his boyish smile flashing sheepishly through his huge shag of shiny, black hormone hair, Elvis looked like a heaping portion of cheesecake ripe for the eye teeth of the hundreds of women ogling him through opera glasses.

Goldman talks of Elvis the superstar of compelling narcissism and then turns to his rapport with the audience. He manages very well with his constituency, "by occasionally grabbing a blue-haired lady at ringside and kissing her firmly on the mouth. Watching the women in the audience lunge toward the stage like salmon up a falls becomes the show's real comic relief."

Of Elvis's singing and musicianship, Goldman says he strums the acoustic guitar with the carelessness of a practised faker and ends every number with a classically struck profile, Elvis as Discus hurler, Elvis as Sagittarius, Elvis as the Dying Gaul.

The climax of Presley's monodrama is a tremendous Cecil B. De Mille tableau. The orchestra is silhouetted against a cerulean blue cyclorama while its members are transfigured by rich gold light pouring in from the wings. As the massed musicians sustain a mighty cathedral chord, the Great White Hope falls on one knee in the classic Jolson-gladiator pose, saluting the thousands in the house.

So here is the image created in Elvis's life. The performance is designed to trigger the same emotions as are triggered by the great swelling sound of cathedral choir and organ. And all in honour of the self-sacrificing gladiator figure offering himself and his body to the audience. One of his favourite costumes for such an occasion was the immensely colourful Aztec Indian design, based on the sun symbols of a civilization and priesthood which required human sacrifice to propitiate the forces of nature. But was Elvis merely manipulating the emotions of a willing audience, triggering the human body into releasing those chemicals and hormones which can produce feelings of ecstasy?

As Elvis neared the end of his days he confided to those close to him that the life he was leading could not continue much longer. He warned his companions, as Christ had done, of his fate. And, during his last concert tour, he spoke to his fans from the stage in a whisper, as if wishing to share a secret with them, to bring them into his confidence, "I am, and I was". Five mysterious words which fans have tried for years to understand.

Some say he was making a reference to the "I am the Alpha and Omega, the first and the last" of the Book of Revelation. Others heard echoes of the God of Israel, Jehovah, "I am who I am". The words could have come from his favourite book, *The Impersonal Life*. It is a twentieth-century work in the esoteric tradition which Elvis kept with him for inspiration throughout the latter years of his life. It starts with a chapter called "I am", and speaks of man as being a manifestation or reflection of the creator's idea. Was Elvis trying to tell his followers that he had discovered God within himself and that he knew the consequences of such a discovery?

At the end of his life many fans believe Elvis was desperate to leave this earth. He had lost his mother, his physical attraction had waned, his friends and companions had betrayed him, and he wanted to find rest from the unhappiness of the world. He prayed to God, it is claimed, not to be allowed to live too many more days. It is said today by fans looking back that he knew the day he was to die: the sixteenth day of the eighth month of the year 1977. As evidence these fans point to the great mystical music of Richard Strauss, *Also Sprach Zarathustra*, which introduced his stage act, known by his followers as 2001, after the film which had made it popular. Add 16 to 8 to 1977 and it equals 2001. Elvis read great significance into numerical coincidences and had a fascination with numerology. Had he also foretold the day of his death? In their enthusiasm to find such coincidences, fans tend to overlook that every month at that time had a date of similar numerical importance. Yet to them his date of death holds the key to understanding the terms on which Elvis faced his end on earth. They are bolstered in that belief by yet further numerical discoveries. Add the day he was born, to the day he died, to the year of his birth and the age at which he died: 8 plus 16 plus 1935 plus 42. What does it make? 2001, of course.

*

During his time of greatest suffering, say his fans, like Jesus, Elvis was betrayed by his friends. Peter denied his Lord and Judas sold him for thirty pieces of silver. Similarly, some of Elvis's closest companions took information about their friend, employer and patron's last days and sold it on the open market to a curious and ghoulish public. It was as if they planned a crucifixion of his image and reputation. It is the part of the Elvis story which still today upsets his devoted followers the most. One writer has even suggested that Elvis committed suicide to avoid the disgrace of being exposed by his closest companions as a drug-dependent, obese "has been" who pigged out on junk food, was doubly incontinent and most of the time barely conscious.

The betrayal of Elvis was by three men who had certainly been among his closest companions: cousins Red and Sonny West and Dave Hebler. Dave Hebler was a karate expert who had been Elvis's bodyguard. For two years he was a loyal member of the "Elvis Mafia", "The Guys", indulging his employer's every whim and, in return, being given extravagant gifts like a $10,000 Mercedes-Benz. He was fired in 1976 after law suits were filed alleging Elvis's bodyguards had acted too zealously in protecting their master.

Red and Sonny had known Elvis much longer. Red had been at High School with Elvis, and a friendship formed when he stepped in to protect the strange schoolkid from bullying. He too was a follower of the martial arts and was nicknamed "The Dragon". He started working for Elvis in 1960. Sonny too had a martial arts nickname, "The Eagle", and he came to live at Graceland on Elvis's staff to look after the singer's large collection of vehicles. Elvis was best man at his wedding in 1971.

Elvis indulged both friends, buying them expensive cars in particular. They in turn protected him. Often criticized for their tough tactics, they kept Elvis safe from a whole variety of hysterical and deranged people. Red West also followed a career as a stuntman, actor and song writer. He appeared in more than a dozen Elvis films.

When the three loyal companions were dismissed they wrote a book about life behind the scenes with Elvis. It was called *Elvis: What Happened?* It hit the bookshelves just before Elvis died and became a bestseller. An early serialized section which appeared in the tabloid press gave the flavour of what was to come. It told the story of Elvis's mad wish to have Priscilla's boyfriend murdered.

Fans viewed the book as a monstrous and inexcusable betrayal. It was, they felt, a public, verbal crucifixion of the man they loved. While his crucifixion did not involve nails being driven through the hands and feet, it did involve metaphorical nails being driven through his pride and vanity and the hearts of his devoted followers. They were shocked to the core about what they read about the real Elvis. Many refused, and still refuse, to believe it. In his book, *Elvis, the Final Years*, Jerry Hopkins describes the book and Elvis's reaction in three pithy paragraphs.

> Suddenly through much of the western world, big headlines and dripping proses chronicled Elvis's abuse of drugs and guns, told of latenight conversations he had with his mother, said he was a man obsessed with religion and psychic powers (his own) and law and order and probable life after death.
>
> The overall picture a reader got was of a fat and stoned-out, ageing rock star locked away in a southern mansion,

venturing forth only on rare occasions to a movie theatre kept open from midnight to dawn for his personal use, living his life by the numbers in his numerology book, a machine gun cradled in his ample lap. Not even Howard Hughes seemed so colourful, so eccentric, so sick.

The book was a distortion, a bitter diatribe without perspective or compassion, motivated by a wish to get even and rich. It was perfect for its gossipy time and perfect in its timing. The book probably wouldn't have attracted so much attention if Elvis hadn't died within a fortnight of its release. Then it sold like hotcakes – nearly three million copies in all. But there was truth in the book – however narrow its scope – and sometimes the truth hurts. Elvis was wounded by it. For hours, day after day, he talked about Red and Sonny and Dave. Dave he could forgive, or forget, he said, because he hadn't been around long. But Red and Sonny were family!

To Billy Stanley, Vernon Presley's stepson, who thought of himself as Elvis's kid brother, the book was "a Judas act".

*

The death of Elvis was a final undignified act. His last hours have been well charted. On the night of 15–16 August, just as he was preparing for yet another tour, Elvis went to sleep never to be seen alive again. He was found the next day by his latest girl friend, Ginger, slumped on the floor of the bathroom. Paramedics were called, Elvis was rushed to the Baptist Memorial Hospital in Memphis, but to no avail. The way his death was handled, and the autopsy which followed, have led to much speculation. Did Elvis commit suicide? Did he die of a heart attack or drug overdose? Certainly a cocktail of prescribed drugs was found in his body. Did he really die? Or was the story of his death just a charade to mask his disappearance from public view?

*

Inevitably there are supernatural legends attached to his death. The origins of most of these legends are hard to trace, but the stories crop up in various guises in conversation with fans. For instance, on the night of Elvis's death, it is said, the lights in the memorial gardens went out quite unaccountably. Another story says that at the time of his death an angel appeared in the clouds above his Memphis home.

The death of Elvis threw many thousands, if not millions, of people into a deep depression. The shock was particularly traumatic in the USA, for many Americans, even though not especially devoted to Elvis, had invested their patriotism in him and his image. He was young, to be admired for his achievements, had served his country uncomplainingly in the army and seemed to be in control of his destiny.

Elvis himself might have had times of self-doubt, but his American public did not. Whatever might have been happening in the world which appeared worrying and uncertain, he and the values he represented were dependable. How could a true American listening to Elvis singing the trilogy doubt that his country was God's own? So when he died the depression was real. Millions of Americans still recall where they were when they heard the news. The event shook the nation. Like the assassination of President Kennedy and the explosion of the space shuttle, it shattered dreams. Afterwards hundreds of people needed to be helped through the shock with counselling, some of which developed into longterm programmes of psychological help. And even when all the lurid details of his last months and his drug dependence became known, people remained loyal. They did not blame him for his death, but rather his doctors and entourage. In one sense he was seen as the sacrifice. In a more mystical way his death was an atonement, a propitiation. It came at a time of a collective American self-doubt. The Vietnam war and the civil rights struggle was still a live memory. America had much on its conscience. Ordinary Americans were beginning to realize that the bright hope of the American dream had its tarnished flipside.

33

Having been the epitome of the upbeat American dream, with his death, many Americans discovered that Elvis epitomized that tarnished, discredited flipside. Elvis was a true product of his culture and his times.

At the time of his death many Americans – and others in the western world who, through the influence of American mass culture, aspired to the American dream – were troubled. They faced changes and uncertain times. Values were being challenged. They were being made to feel the old ways had been wrong. Consumption, materialism, gas-guzzling, unquestioning patriotism were open to question. The way to appease a conscience is through sacrifice: the gesture made to God or the gods, the symbol of atonement. The death of Elvis served the purpose.

There is another dimension to this idea of Elvis's death being an atonement. That which is sacrificed must be innocent. It is taught that Christ, the ultimate sacrifice, was without sin. In early Judaism, the sacrifices offered in the temple were blameless goats and lambs. Elvis too is now seen by his fans as being innocent of his own death. There was a mystique about him, and, despite his excesses in life, his fans forgive him his faults and blame his doctors and companions for bringing about his end. Some fans even blame themselves for having made such demands on their hero that he was unable to stand up to the pressure.

There were two distinct sides to Elvis. There was the humble, clean-cut boy who addressed ladies as "ma'am" and was the true American gentleman. Then there was the foul-mouthed, truculent, spoiled brat, gun-toting Elvis who fancied and had any inexperienced young girl he chose. The fans honour the first Elvis and forgive the human frailties of the second. Some fans say the first Elvis was the true Elvis, but he lived his life in tension, wrestling with the spirit of his twin, Jesse Garon, for control of his earthly body. In him was the universal struggle between good and evil. Even Christ, the fans say, first in the wilderness, then later in the Garden of Gethsemane and finally at the height of his suffering and passion, had to endure that conflict within himself. So, they would say, it was the innocent, the good side of Elvis which was sacrificed. The Elvis of the Elvis myth is the innocent party, the cleaned up version of the real thing. And the myth is encapsulated as the epitaph on his grave at Graceland.

Beneath his name and dates are written words chosen by Vernon Presley:

He was a precious gift from God we cherished and loved dearly. He had a God-given talent that he shared with the world, and without doubt he became most widely acclaimed, capturing the hearts of young and old alike. He was admired not only as an entertainer, but as the great humanitarian that he was, for his generosity and his kind feelings for his fellow man. He revolutionized the field of music and received its highest awards. He became a living legend in his own time, earning the respect and love of millions. God saw that he needed some rest and called him home to be with him. We miss you, son and daddy. I thank God that he gave us you as our son.

When followers of Elvis came to him and called him the King, he rebuked them saying, "No, don't think like this. There is only one King, and that is Jesus." Since his death his fans have gone unrebuked.

TWO

☆

The Message

Elvis was a star of the electronic age. The family Bible in the home which once took pride of place in the living room and was opened every night for study and prayer, is now replaced by the family television set. Millions of people today are far more at ease listening to records and radios, than reading a book.

So, if nothing else, Elvis can lay claim to being the first prophet of the era of electronic image and sound. It is an era in which people are absorbing ideas and images in short sound-bites and fast-moving, ever-changing quasi-hypnotic images. There is demand for immediate answers and instant emotional and philosophical gratification. Elvis meets the need. At the flick of a switch, or the press of a button on the video remote control gadget, he is there, singing of love, loneliness, jealousy, hope or God. If Elvis has left behind his equivalent of a scripture, it is not to be found inscribed on pages and bound in black leather, it is to be found in his enormous legacy of recordings, films and videos of shows. And it is to the lyrics of his songs that his fans look in particular for inspiration.

Elvis recorded a huge repertoire of songs. He was not a major composer of his own material like Bob Dylan or John Lennon, although he was largely responsible for a number of his hits and made amendments and contributed ideas to many other songs to suit his own approach. His choice of material reflects both his own taste and that of his musical and commercial advisers; and because the range of music is so wide it is almost always possible for a fan looking to Elvis for solace or inspiration to find the right off-the-peg emotion. A fan wishing to feel the warmth of the voice of Elvis singing to her as if she were the only woman he loved, would seek out a recording of *Love Me Tender*, *The Hawaiian Wedding Song*, or *Pledging My Love*. If jealousy is the problem, what more appropriate song than *Suspicious Minds*? Or if the pain of broken love needs soothing, there are many lyrics to choose from like "I'm hurt to think you lied to me . . . I'm hurt more than you'll ever know." Or, "Love has slipped away and left us only friends." Elvis fans say, echoing the words of many Christians, it is possible not only to love Elvis, but to be loved by Elvis and have a personal relationship with him.

A common theme in his songs is loneliness. Elvis sings to his listeners in such a way as to say, "I understand what loneliness is like." "I get so lonely, baby. I get so lonely, I could die," is the refrain from *Heartbreak Hotel*, which talks of being "Down at the end of lonely street at heartbreak hotel". In *Don't Be Cruel* Elvis conjures up images both of loneliness and rejection:

> You know I can be found, sitting home all alone.
> If you can't come around,
> At least please telephone,
> Don't be cruel to a heart that's true.

Or again, the song *Kentucky Rain* starts, "Seven lonely days and a dozen towns to go." And again in *A Mess of Blues*, Elvis sings, "I swear I'm going crazy, sitting here all alone. Since you're gone, I'm a mess of blues." The theme recurs in so many guises. "Loneliness is darkness's first companion . . . Spend a night alone and faith may bend." Or, "It's a lonely man who roams from town to town, searchin', searchin', for something he can't find." Not forgetting, of course, the huge 1960 Elvis Presley hit, number one in the American charts for six weeks, *Are You Lonesome Tonight?*

Is your heart filled with pain, Shall I come back again?
Tell me dear, are you lonesome tonight?

Another theme is life at the rough end. It is part of the "poor
boy made good who does not forget his roots" image. So in
My Way, Elvis sings of the pride he has taken in following
the independent line in life. The song *Poor Boy* contains the
verse:

Ain't got a crust,
Ain't got a cent,
Can't buy a jug,
Can't pay the rent.
I got a heart full of dreams and a lot of memories,
And that's enough for me.

And the most evocative of Elvis's songs in which he conjures
up the picture of poverty and deprivation he knew is *In the
Ghetto*. To begin with the listener is deceived into thinking
that the words have a Christian nativity meaning behind them:
"As the snow flies, on a cold and grey Chicago mornin', a poor
little baby child is born, in the ghetto." Yet the song takes an
unexpected twist: "The child needs a helping hand, or he'll grow
to be an angry young man some day." It reaches an angry
climax:

And then one night in desperation, a young man
    breaks away,
He buys a gun, steals a car, tries to run, but he don't
    get far,
And his mama cries.

The song finishes on a note of helplessness. It reinforces the
idea that poverty is a cycle of desperation. It contradicts the
American dream which Elvis himself has lived out. Elvis must
have known how close he came to being the boy in his song
and that it was not his doing which lifted him away from the

normal poverty trap. Is he saying that he was lifted from it for a purpose by God or by the good luck of having a rare set of vocal chords? Whatever the answer to that question, Elvis was certainly re-emphasizing that part of his image which said, "I might be poor boy made good, but I have not forgotten where I came from and what I might have been".

> As her young man dies,
> On a cold and grey Chicago mornin' another little
>   baby is born,
> In the ghetto.
> And his mama cries . . .

In *Jailhouse Rock*, Elvis not only shows an empathy for those who have found themselves on the wrong side of the law, but adds a dignity to their situation, by singing of them as individuals. Elvis perhaps had it in mind that his own father had spent time in gaol when he was young, on a dud cheque charge. The song came from the film of the same name, the third Elvis made. It is now generally thought to be the best, or at least the most interesting and original, film constructed for him. In it Elvis played the part of a prisoner serving time for killing a man in a bar. When in prison, he finds and develops a talent for singing. As in many of his films, part of the Presley myth is moulded into a story line and used for its entertainment value.

*

Through his songs Elvis also raises the hopes of the lonely and the less fortunate. If worldly success and fortune are not forthcoming, there is comfort to be had in the life to come:

> Tho' often tempted, tormented and tested,
> And like the prophet, my pillow a stone;
> And tho' I find here no permanent dwelling,
> I know He'll give me a mansion of my own.
> I've got a mansion, just over the hilltop,

In that bright land where we'll never grow old;
And some day yonder we will never more wander,
But walk on streets that are purest gold.

A similar message is to be drawn from the gospel song *Farther Along*:

Tempted and tried we're oft made to wonder,
Why it should be thus all the day long;
While there are others living about us,
Never molested tho' in the wrong . . .
When we see Jesus coming in glory,
When He comes from His home in the sky;
Then we shall meet Him in that bright mansion,
We'll understand it all by and by.

In his younger days, of course, much of Elvis's appeal was in the raw sexuality of his talent. He was then seen as the rebel, a threat to the morals of the young. The finer, delicate lyrics of the love songs of the forties and fifties, were turned into such lines as, "I'm in love, I'm all shook up", or, "Just a big hunk of love will do", or "Girls, big and brassy, girls small and sassy, just give me one of each kind", even, by 1965, "Hang a sign on the door, do not disturb, it's time to make love, I can't wait any more."

Later Elvis became respectable, a symbol of the American dream. He served in the armed forces, met the president and declared his patriotism through his music. His *American Trilogy* is a medley of three songs, *Dixie*, *All My Trials* and *The Battle Hymn of the Republic*, which have deeply felt associations. "Mine eyes have seen the glory of the coming of the Lord . . . Glory, glory, Alleluia", was sung at the funeral of Robert Kennedy and the inauguration of President Lyndon Johnson. Wayne Newton performed the song at the Republican convention in 1980 which nominated Ronald Reagan as presidential candidate. To many Americans the words and images of the three songs revive an incomparable, nostalgic yearning to believe that America is good and was set on its path to greatness by God Himself. Though other possible interpretations should not be overlooked: was Elvis, like Christ, foretelling his destiny in the hushed words from *All My Trials*, "Now, hush little darlin', don't you cry. You know your Daddy's bound to die."

*

Of all his recordings it is the overtly religious music which his long time fans say they turn to most. The other music, for all its vibrancy and intimacy, could have been, and often was, performed by other singers. In many cases they have been singers who have, or have had, their own armies of fans, but who have never acquired the status of Elvis: not even those who died young – John Lennon, James Dean, Freddie Mercury, Buddy Holly or Billy Fury. It is perhaps because Elvis has this status, with all its religious overtones, that his gospel music is singled out by his fans for special mention. Though it must not be forgotten that gospel music was also Elvis's first love, in that he grew up with the Christian music of the southern United States, and was familiar with most of the standard tunes and words before encountering rock and roll.

It is ironic that the raunchy pop star whose girating pelvis was once banned from American television, helped bring the traditional hymn *Amazing Grace* to a wide secular audience.

> Amazing Grace how sweet the sound,
> That saved a wretch like me!
> I once was lost, but now am found,
> Was blind, but now I see.

And his song *Let Us Pray* was first heard in the film *Change of Habit* released in 1970. In it Elvis, playing the part of a doctor working in a slum clinic, falls in love with one of the nuns working with him. The film presents the nun, played by Mary Tyler Moore, with the dilemma: choose Elvis or religious vocation. The song has a straightforward Catholic evangelical beat.

Come praise the Lord for He is good.
Come join in love and brotherhood,
We'll hear the "Word" and bring our gifts of bread
   and wine,
And we'll be blessed beneath His sign.

The song *Peace in the Valley* had been a major million selling
record long before Elvis chose to sing it on The Ed Sullivan
Show. It had been composed in 1939 by a Reverend Thomas
Dorsey, inspired by the scenery he had viewed from the window
of a train travelling from Indiana to Cincinnati. Elvis inevitably
interpreted the song in his unique way. The words have a direct
religious meaning. When heard by today's fans, they reinforce
for them the spiritual nature of the Elvis story.

   I am tired and weary but I must toil on,
   Till the Lord comes to call me away.

The third verse is a direct biblical reference:

   There the bear will be gentle, the wolf will be tame,
   And the lion will lay down by the lamb.

The refrain finishes:

   I pray no more sorrow and sadness or trouble will be,
   There'll be peace in the valley for me.

And are there hidden religious meanings to be read into even
the most seemingly irreligious numbers? Is there an echo of
the exclusive road to salvation offered by Christ discernible
in the words of one version of *Hound Dog*? "You'll never get
to heaven, if you ain't no friend of mine" is how one line sounds.
It is perhaps stretching a point to suggest it. The song originally
was an all powerful shocker which had an older generation
quaking. It was a challenge to youth to declare their social
independence, to take decisions for themselves and not blindly

follow their elders into making all the same mistakes as the previous generation, mistakes which had led to depression and war. The song has not mellowed over the years, but the teenagers who first heard it are now parents and grandparents themselves. They were challenged to rethink their lives when they first heard the music. They now have the chance to find new meanings in the words, religious ones perhaps. Instant spiritual gratification, if it is to have any lasting value, needs to turn into a deeper spiritual exploration of self and purpose.

And what might a devotee, sitting with her Elvis collection, think when her recording of *Just Pretend* is turning on the record player? Christ's message to His followers was, "I am with you always". Elvis's words are, "Just pretend I'm holding you, and whisp'ring things soft and low. And think of me . . . just pretend I didn't go. Just pretend I'm right there with you . . ."

> I'll come flying to you again,
> All the crying is through.
> I will hold you and love you again,
> But until then, we'll just pretend.

While in many of Elvis's films a rather mawkish stereotype of good triumphs over a rather unconvincing image of bad, his music does sometimes go further. In rather a sugary way, it does introduce ideas of forgiveness and redemption. For religious sentimentality, *Crying in the Chapel* is hard to beat.

> Every sinner looks for something,
> That will put his heart at ease;
> There is only one true answer,
> He must get down on his knees.

Although it is closely matched by *He*:

> He can turn the tides and calm the angry sea.
> He alone decides who writes a symphony.

He lights every star that makes our darkness bright.
He keeps watch all through each long and lonely night.
He still finds the time to hear a child's first prayer,
Saint or sinner call and always find him there.
Though it makes him sad to see the way we live,
He'll always say, "I forgive".

And on the other side of the *Crying in the Chapel* single released in 1965 is a number called *I Believe in the Man in the Sky*: "I believe with his help, I'll get by."

A number of Elvis's popular religious songs did not become major chart successes. *We Call on Him*, for instance, was never a chart success, and yet some sources claim that, over time, it sold a million copies. The song is a simple statement of faith in God as protector.

*

Elvis also makes reference, without qualification or apology, to various popular superstitions. The rabbit's foot for luck is one and in *A Big Hunk O'Love*, he refers to his lucky charms. In fact he recorded a song called *Good Luck Charm*. In *Mean Woman Blues* there is the line, "A black cat up and died of fright, 'cause she crossed his path last night." His recording *I Got Lucky* runs through the whole gamut of modern good luck objects from four leaf clovers to horse shoes to magic wishing trees. For anyone looking for a satanic influence behind Elvis's music, his songs *Devil in Disguise* and *Witchcraft* might provide some interest, although the former could easily be interpreted either as the song of a disillusioned lover or a warning to Christians to be wary of diabolic deception.

> You look like an angel,
> Walk like an Angel,
> Talk like an Angel,
> But I got wise;
> You're the Devil in disguise.

There is a curious song which Elvis recorded, called *Flaming Star*. It is curious in the respect that it heralds some of the debate concerning Elvis's death. There are those who feel that Elvis, if he did not actually commit suicide or deliberately will his death, foretold his own end. It can almost be said that he had a control over his death, had dominion over it, conquered it even, by being able to determine the time. *Flaming Star* suggests that he was, even as early as 1960, aware of the direction his life was leading him. His mother was dead and he was still grieving. The song is the title track from a film in which Elvis plays the part of a half-Indian. The story is set in the great never-never land of the American wild west. At the end of the film, Elvis, who is near to death, announces he is going to ride to the mountains to die an Indian, as he has seen the flaming star of death.

> Every man has a flaming star, a flaming star over his
> shoulder.
> And when a man sees his flaming star, he knows his
> time has come.
> Flaming Star don't you shine on me.
> Flaming Star, keep behind a me.

The final album released in Elvis's lifetime was the enigmatic *Moody Blue*. Fans knowing of Elvis's interest in numerology, particularly in the way he might have used it to plan or foretell his death, could read a great deal of significance into the lyrics. They could be seen to be endorsing numerology and encouraging fans to look to the "art" for signs.

> Well, it's hard to be a gambler, bettin' on the number
> that changes every time,
> Well, you think you gonna win, think she's givin' in,
> a stranger you will find,
> Yeah, it's hard to figure out, what she's all about,
> she's a woman through and through,
> She's a complicated lady, so colour my baby, moody blue.

Added meaning could be read into the song when it is recalled that Elvis's favourite colour was supposed to be blue and at the beginning of his life, a mysterious blue light had signalled his arrival. Fanciful stuff, but where Elvis is concerned there is always someone willing to give credence to such notions.

Elvis presents his fans with choice. In *Any Way You Want Me* he uses the line, "In your hands my heart is clay, to take and mould as you may . . . "I'll be a fool or a wiseman, my darling, you hold the key." In *Puppet on a String*, he says, "You can do most anything with me." And *Wild in the Country*, offers another option, to picture Elvis as an allegory of creation:

> A rose grows wild in the country,
> A tree grows tall as the sky,
> The wind blows wild in the country,
> And part of the wild, wild country am I.

A final song is worth mentioning, for it was the last hit single Elvis recorded and meanings have been read into the words which suggest that Elvis knew of the nature of his death and how his body would be discovered. The words were not the composer's original choice, but Elvis's own variation:

> Fate is growing closer,
> And look at my resistance,
> Found lying on the floor,
> Taking me to places that I've never been before.

Much of what fans feel Elvis is saying to them comes both from the lyrics and from the intimacy of the sound or the raw excitement he engendered. His music covers the spectrum of emotion and expresses the feelings ordinary fans experience. One fan put it this way. She was not an obsessive follower of the King, she did not wear Elvis badges or plaster her house with Elvis pictures. She had a catholic taste in music, sometimes listening to classical music, sometimes to other pop, and to other rock 'n' roll besides Elvis. She said, "If I come home and have had a bad day, I can put an Elvis record on and he can change my mood. I have a favourite saying, 'Music washes away from the soul the dust of everyday life'. That is what Elvis's music does for me."

*

While many dedicated Elvis fans have videos and can buy copies of his films to watch at home, and one motel opposite Graceland in Memphis boasts that it plays Elvis films twenty-four hours a day in all the rooms, the Elvis films are, in the main, less popular than both his records and the videos of his live performances and television shows. It is even recognized by Elvis fans that although their idol spent much of his working life on the movie set, he made few really memorable films. The movies were made largely at the insistence of Elvis's manager Colonel Tom Parker, to earn quick money. The plots were often thin and the acting weak. The Elvis message, as portrayed in the films, is by and large shallow. Some are simple "boy meets girl" stories; others do make an attempt to convey a simple moral, but they are rarely more than commercial pot-boilers, or launching pads for records. A common theme is a rerun of the great American dream or myth that poor boy can make good if he behaves himself, works hard, is loyal to Uncle Sam and is handy with his fists (if provoked). Despite the numbers of films he made, averaging two a year between 1956 and 1970, and the time he spent in front of the camera, his film work has contributed very little to his subsequent image and appeal. Elvis is the superhero he is today despite his films, not because of them. There are moments in the films which fans cherish. Sometimes a flashed smile, a laugh, a witty line, a glance stands out, and for a few seconds Elvis transcends the mediocrity of the plot. Of all his work, the films are the most criticized. Some fans staunchly defend them, as they defend any attack on his reputation. It is "TCE" they say, "Taking Care of Elvis". But even the most devoted followers admit the films have little of substance. Good light entertainment, is how they are described.

The message of Elvis, as understood by one of his most devoted present day followers, is not one of great profundity or mystical wisdom. It is a repetition of simple virtues and values. "Nothing we have now will we have when we leave this earth. So be generous and compassionate and love people. Elvis gave and is still giving love to us. Elvis came from God because we needed somebody. It was about the time. A lot of people had strayed away from God and God could have come and dramatically called us to Him; but instead He chose to send Elvis. He was a humble boy who spoke to us through his music, his feelings, his actions, his giving and the way he helped people.

"Many people have said to me that Elvis brought them back to God, or led them back to church again, or brought about a change for the good. No one has become a drug addict because of Elvis. His influence has been to the good. Nobody has come to me to say that Elvis had helped them to be bad. In the way that people were sent to see and hear Jesus in Jerusalem, some superpower sends people to Elvis."

THREE

☆

Give Up All and
Follow Me

Kiki Apostolakos

Early, almost every morning, long before the fans arrive
at Graceland in their hundreds, a lone figure arrives at the
gate and walks slowly up the drive. She is a tall, dignified
woman with black hair. Often she carries flowers. She has
the bearing of a widow on her way to tend a dead husband's
grave.

Kiki Apostolakos is well known to all the long-serving staff
at Elvis's home, she is seen so frequently standing by the singer's
grave, deep in thought. Sometimes at her early morning vigil
she is joined by other Elvis fans who have discovered that in
the quiet, just after daybreak, they can spend time at the grave
undisturbed by the hosts of daytime visitors. Kiki is a fan who
has devoted her life to Elvis. Like Marie Mappley, Dorothy
Smith, Val Quinn, Jennifer Walker, Leslie Stanek, Sid Shaw,
Pam and Aaron Richie and the many others whose stories will
be told, her whole life is focused on Elvis.

Fifteen years ago, living in her home country of Greece and
working as a teacher of psychology, Kiki would not have
described herself as an Elvis fan. She knew his music, but
thought little more of it than the music of the many other pop
stars of the era. However the unexpected announcement of the
death of Elvis triggered such a deep emotional response that

she left her family and native country to live in Memphis and dedicate her life to the memory of the King.

It was seven o'clock in the morning on a Friday in August 1977. I was at the sink in the kitchen of my house having had coffee with my mother and I was listening to the radio. Suddenly a lady came on and said the programme was being interrupted for the news that the King of Rock and Roll was with us no more. It was as if something hit my head. Something crashed inside me. I turned to the radio and said, "No, this can't be possible!" The cups in my hand fell into the sink. My mother heard the noise. "What's going on?" she said. "Why are you talking to yourself?" I told her that Elvis had passed away. "Who is Elvis anyway?" she said. I had one record of his which I had been given and showed it to her. "This is Elvis" I said, "He was so young."

From that day I was like a robot. I had no appetite for anything. Only my job gave me any interest. I kept asking myself, why am I living? What can I expect in life now? I began to think of how I could get to the United States and to Memphis. I put Elvis pictures up in my room. I was at the time divorcing my first husband. Two or three times when he came to the house to see the children, my daughters, he ran into my room and tried to tear down the pictures. I was so mad I ripped the sleeve from his shirt.

A year after that he stole my kids and I started to pray, "Please God, help me to find my kids and to go to Memphis." The two things I wanted. "Please, if it's not possible to find my kids, please make it possible to go to Memphis."

Kiki's chance to go to Memphis came as a result of meeting the man who was to become her second husband. At the time she had no intention of remarrying, wishing only to dedicate her life to the memory of Elvis. A friend however introduced her to a Greek American, Steve, who worked at the US Embassy. Kiki told him of her ambition to visit America and Memphis in particular.

After two or three months he said he was in love with me and asked me to marry him and go to the United States with him. But I said I didn't want to get married, I wanted to be by myself. He asked me to think about it. I said I would marry him, travel to Memphis and then divorce him. He said, no, he wanted to spend the rest of his life with me. He kept pressing me. It was as if he was being put up to it. At that time I didn't think it was part of a plan. But maybe it was what I had been praying for.

Steve took Kiki first on a ten day trip to the USA.

We went to Memphis and I stood in front of Elvis's grave. I was so strong, I didn't cry at all the first time. But I knew he was there so close. I had cried so much, maybe I had no more tears left to cry. It was strange. The first day we went walking around Memphis and we passed by a funeral home. I knew instinctively that it was there that Elvis had been taken. I went in to ask. Then, by chance, we saw the Baptist Memorial Hospital he had been taken to. It was as if we were being guided. We had booked in at a hotel, not knowing where in Memphis it was. We then discovered a bus left for Graceland from right outside the door! We spent ten days getting to know Memphis. Then back to Greece.

Kiki decided to marry Steve as her way of returning to Memphis to live. Her parents were shocked. They felt she was more in love with Elvis than her new husband.

My father did not say goodbye, my mother the same. She said, "You forget from this moment that you have parents and other relatives." I told them, no problem. They said, how would I manage if anything went wrong, and I was in a strange country. I said that God would protect me, He knew why I was going and had helped me to go to Memphis. They said, not even Elvis's wife does the things I do. I didn't even know the man or meet him. But it is what you feel,

I said. "Did you ever meet Jesus?" I asked my mother. "No, of course not," she said, "we haven't met him but we believe in him and love him. But Jesus", said my mother, "is a God." I told her, "All right. But we didn't meet the apostles or the saints and yet we believe in them and love them. They weren't Gods. After God, in my heart," I told my mother, "I have all you, my family and Elvis together. He is part of the family. I know him. I am forty-one. I have done what you have wanted me to do, now is the time to do what I want to do. I love you, but the time has come for me to go where I know I will be happy." "But what will you do," they said, "just go to the graveside and cry for Elvis all day? You will die. You are going to leave your parents for someone who is dead." "He is not dead for me," I said, "not dead for me."

I tried to phone them from the airport but the maid answered the phone and they didn't come. But when I arrived I wrote to them regularly and in the third year they began to write to me. And after my mother came here she saw that I was happy and said I should continue with what I was doing.

When Steve, Kiki's second husband, died, she stayed on in Memphis, her devotion to Elvis as strong as ever. She supports herself by working as a waitress and gives every spare moment of her life to Elvis. She keeps fresh flowers on his grave and tidies away the dead leaves. When at home in her apartment, just off Elvis Presley Boulevard, she listens to Elvis's music and watches videos of his films and stage performances. Every room in her apartment has souvenirs of Elvis. In her bedroom a large wall poster of the King has been placed alongside a picture of Christ. The two appear to be looking at each other.

Kiki talks of going to the graveside as if she was going to a church. She prays for Elvis and for his family, mother, father, grandmother and twin brother all buried or remembered in the meditation garden at Graceland.

I pray for all mankind and I thank God for helping me to be here. As I pray I think, "Here he comes," it is time for him to step out. His image is so alive inside me. I meet so many people, men and women, at the graveside and many write to me later and ask me to send a prayer to Elvis for them. I talk to him in my mind. I feel very comfortable. I tell him what I feel, that I miss him. I talk about friends who send money to me to buy flowers. I tell Elvis that his friends are still thinking about him and will be back to be by the grave when they can. I share worries and problems. I don't pray to Elvis, he was a human being. I don't accept what some people say that he is God. If he was God he would be at a distance. There is a distance between human beings and God. That is why we are close to Elvis. He is like a bridge between us and God.

I don't pray to Elvis but to God. Then, here comes Elvis in my dreams. But I am not asleep. But here he comes. It gives me an answer to what I am waiting for, in my problem. I had a dream when people started damaging his grave. I saw the pieces of marble and the next time I came up I saw what had happened. I had had a premonition, a warning from Elvis.

Kiki describes each morning as a fresh experience, as if, she says, she was going to be with Elvis for the first time. "I feel like a child going to meet someone exciting for the first time". When she leaves the graveside each time she follows a routine of action and prayer. She crosses herself, as she would on entering or leaving a church, and bends down to kiss the grave of Elvis by briefly touching her lips with her hand and then conveying the kiss to the ground. She reassures Elvis that she will be back and wishes him happiness. She asks him too to pray to God for everyone who has him in their heart.

Kiki then takes a short bus ride north towards the centre of Memphis to her home. There she makes sure the house is filled with his music. Listening to it, she says, it is like no other music. "When I put his gospel songs on, I feel a shiver inside me. He talks to us through his music." Kiki believes she will remain in love with Elvis, living near to his grave and meditating in the grounds of Graceland, for the rest of her life. If she has to return to Greece for brief visits she makes arrangements for a friend to tend the grave and renew the flowers in her absence. To make up for any lost time away, Kiki sometimes spends the whole night at Graceland. She will bring food, some for herself and some for the security guards. If she cannot go in to be by the grave, she sits across the street, looking at Graceland. Then as dawn breaks she goes to collect flowers to take to the grave as soon as the gates open. There are times when Kiki does not sleep in her bed for three or four days. She leaves her job and goes straight to Graceland for an all night vigil.

"It is not only me," Kiki stresses, even though she admits she might have more stamina than many fans and a greater opportunity to be by Elvis's grave. "There are many people like me. They wish they could live here in Memphis. They say I must be so proud. And I am." Kiki admits that for all the time she spends by Elvis's grave, she spends very little time by the grave of her husband, the man who made it possible for her to fulfil her dream. When still alive he had asked her if she would, if he died, spend time at his grave. She admitted to him that while she was dedicated to looking after him, she did not love him as she loved Elvis. Hers was a special love for Elvis. Today she is firm in her determination not to marry again. Many men have propositioned her. One even said that she should close her eyes while he made love to her and imagine being in the arms of Elvis. Kiki refused. She knew she could not deceive herself. She remains faithful to her one true love, Elvis.

When I was with my second husband, he was nice, I had to do something because he was my husband, but I didn't feel comfortable. Now I wonder why I did it, I didn't have to, but it was good for him. Now I only think of Elvis. I am dead sexually. It doesn't bother me. I feel I am being faithful to Elvis. Sometimes I dream or imagine I am close to Elvis. I don't know what other people do, but I don't imagine I am making love with Elvis. He didn't make love with every woman he came close to, but he could still make a woman feel special just by talking. When I wake up from thinking I am with Elvis, I think it is not a dream. It is too vivid. I call out to him. To me it is very natural.

Being close to Elvis, Kiki believes is her purpose. It is the answer to her prayers to God. She is in Memphis to honour Elvis and to help others who come to Memphis to get to know the places Elvis knew. "Everyone has a purpose," she says, "but I feel special, because Elvis makes me feel this way. I have so much love and support in what I am doing." Sometimes the staff at Graceland put her in touch with visitors needing help. Not long ago she met two German girls who wanted to plan a return visit, but had little chance of affording both fare and accommodation. Kiki told them, if they could manage to buy the tickets, she would look after them in Memphis, they could stay with her. "If it is for him," she told them, "come and stay as long as you want. " Kiki saw it as her way of thanking God for answering her prayers.

It is human, she says, to go where your heart leads and stay where you heart wishes to stay. It is when people reject their instincts and inner wishes and yearnings, she says, that people are restless and unhappy.

My interest in Elvis grows every day, but I do no harm, I am not dangerous. I am a quiet person. I don't bother anybody and feel peaceful and calm inside and growing a better human being every day. I am not ashamed of what I feel or believe. They tell me I am obsessed, that I seem so much alive as a person and yet so dedicated to a dead man.

In some ways Kiki has opted for a life similar to that of a woman who takes a religious vow. She lives in relative poverty, or at least at a standard of living far lower than one she could attain. She has chosen faithfulness and obedience to the memory of Elvis. For many centuries it has been common for women who have married and raised children to seek to devote the second half of their life to a religious principle, or some ideal purpose. This could be said to be true for Kiki. Other people opt to forgo marriage and worldly interests at a far younger age. Writing in a fan magazine in 1984 a fan from Yorkshire wrote, "I know many 100% real fans who have told me they would never marry or have children because they could never give up a 100% Elvis life, and they are the real FANS!"

Marie Mappley

Marie Mappley is like many thousands of Elvis fans who, while totally dedicated to Elvis, can visit Graceland only when time and finances allow. She lives in Middlesex and vividly recalls the first time, when she was ten years old, she heard the Elvis sound. It was in the mid-nineteen fifties and she heard her first Elvis record on her father's stereogram via an American radio station broadcasting in Europe.

I took to his voice straight away. I recognized the voice when I heard it again. I enjoyed his style of music and went to find his record in the shops. That started me out on collecting everything. Every single, album, legal and bootleg recording. I got a part-time job in a record shop while I was still at school, so that I would have the money ready to get every Elvis recording that came out. In over thirty-five years collecting I have spent a fortune; sometimes £50 or £80 a record for something rare. I was buying books too, and later videos. My collection is now worth a lot of money, but I would never sell it. Many of the records are on their original labels, which to a fellow collector gives them even greater value.

Marie first saw what her idol looked like when she saw a picture in a girl's magazine. She cut it out and kept it on her desk lid at school. Later she bought other things with his picture, ranging from rings to bottles of scent. Today she has a whole cabinet devoted to his records and a special place in her house where Elvis is particularly remembered. She goes to as many of the British fan conventions as she can and meets with fellow fans to play his music and talk about the King of Rock and Roll. She describes the day she heard of the death of Elvis as the worst of her life. Friends at work kept the news from her as they knew it would upset her, and her husband broke the news. But that was not until the next morning when he phoned Marie from his work.

He asked me if I was OK. I said, yes, but wondered why he had really phoned. He said, "Have you got the radio on?" Then something inside me clicked. "It's Elvis, isn't it? He's dead, isn't he?" He said, yes, he had seen it in the papers as he was going to work.

That is the first time I knew. I was devastated. I had to carry on because I had a young baby. But for a week I couldn't go to work. Even for a whole year after that, if people said anything to me about Elvis, I would fill up and I would break down.

It still happens from time to time. When we are on our Elvis holidays and I am with fans, especially during American Trilogy with all the movement and actions. I get a lump in my throat and feel so emotional. I am in love with Elvis. I have been in love with him since I was ten years old. He has been my entire life. Nothing else has mattered as long as I could get to an Elvis function, buy a record, see a film. I love Elvis. My family shares me with him. My husband isn't an Elvis fan. He knew when he married me he was marrying me and Elvis. He has accepted that. He has never stopped me going anywhere and often takes me to and collects me from functions. My son has his own tastes in music. He has never known his mother any different.

Elvis People
Dorothy Smith

Dorothy Smith who lives in the neighbouring state keeps coming back to Graceland to be in touch with her memories of Elvis. She was one of the thousands of fans who gathered outside the gates of her hero's home the day he died and stayed and stayed. She was also one of the hundreds allowed to view Elvis's body. Her memories of the time she heard the announcement of his death are as vivid as any cherished by his fans. Like those who recall exactly what they were doing when they heard of President Kennedy's death, she has the moment she learned of Elvis's passing etched on her mind.

My heart was just broke. I had lost the best there was. The world had lost the best singer there ever was. He was just great. I just cried, I couldn't believe he was gone. I heard the news on the radio. My daughter and I were on the way to a dentist appointment. We did a U-turn in the road and drove to Graceland. We stayed there all day, and through the night. We were standing by the gates. The people kept just coming and coming. The crowds got bigger and bigger. I thought I wouldn't move. I would just stay there and see. See what? I don't know what I thought I would see. I couldn't miss it. I had to be there. There were thousands. Way up the street.

When his body came back they were letting people in, twenty-five or thirty at a time to view it. My son-in-law, my daughter and I went. I just couldn't believe it was him. I know it was him, but I couldn't bring myself to think he was gone. And I could see that he was him and it hurt so bad. I just didn't like it at all. I am positive it was him. I had just gone to a concert, a couple or three months before he passed away. He had put on a lot of weight. He was real big. I knew it was him. I had seen him just a few months before that. It was him.

When British fan Val Quinn, her daughter Justine and a friend Kathy Baker made a trip to Memphis, they did not return to Britain. According to the fan magazine *Elvisly Yours*, they stayed in the city, planning to start a small business to help support themselves and be near everything that was associated with Elvis. The magazine called it , "a brave decision . . . the sort of decision thousands of British fans would like to make but never pluck up the courage." Over the years there has been a steady trickle of dedicated fans who have made the move, with varying degrees of success. Jennifer Walker comes originally from Devon. Today she and her daughter Maria, who is twenty, live in Memphis in a house just off Elvis Presley Boulevard and a few minutes from Graceland.

We came here because of Elvis. I have been an Elvis fan since I was eleven years old. We came here, got in with the Elvis thing, made good friends, bought a house and we are here.

We are into charitable and civic activities for Elvis at the high school. There are a lot of deprived kids there. We hope to do more. We get together and talk about the old days, watch Elvis videos and meet interesting people from overseas. We go once a week to Graceland. He was so dear to us and a landmark in so many people's lives. A lot of love and friendships are made through Elvis.

Maria was too young to have known of Elvis when he was alive, but finds him an inspiring figure. She goes with her mother to Graceland and says she is particularly moved by the memorial service and candlelit vigil in August. "It is so quiet, peaceful. It has a religious feeling to it."

The day of Elvis's death is clearly etched in Jennifer's mind. Maria was staying with her grandmother in England at the time and Jennifer was working in Washington DC.

I came home to my little bedsit studio apartment thinking I would have a nice quiet dinner. I switched on the TV. The first words I heard were, ". . . and we'll have more on the death of Elvis Presley after the break." I had a cold feeling inside me. Tears streamed down my face. I wasn't such an Elvis fan then as I am now. But something in my life had gone. It hasn't been replaced to this day.

He was a strongly spiritual man, right through to the end. The more I stay in Memphis and meet people who knew him, the more I feel that. He has got so many people loving him, and that is not too strong a word, that he is being drawn closer to the earth.

Jennifer dismisses reports of Elvis being seen alive today as stories made up by eccentrics or people wanting to make a buck. But she does not reject the idea that spiritual contact can be made.

I had one very vivid dream once. And in it I felt Elvis touching me. It was one of those dreams after which you wonder, was that a dream or was that real? We don't know enough about the mind to know what really happened.

People like Kiki are close to him spiritually. She's not doing it to escape, because she can't find her own man. She's been married twice and she looks like a Greek fashion model to me. Her house is like a shrine to Elvis and decorated very artistically.

There must have been some purpose to Elvis's life. Maybe it was to bring people together. I have a number of friends with whom I have nothing in common, except Elvis. There is so much hatred in this world, it is nice that there is something other than hatred and cruelty. Elvis brings love and lightness.

And Jennifer has a special memory of Elvis to cherish. In 1976 she attended one of his concerts at the Capital Center, Maryland. By that time, she says,

he had lost some of his matinee good looks and I was seventy-five yards away from him, but the concert was everything

I had expected. Even after his illness began, he was always Elvis, even though touring must have been a strain on him. People didn't realise the extent of the strain, the death threats, the cruelty. When his marriage broke up it was headlines. He couldn't sort things out privately.

Anyway, as he was announced at the concert, even before the compere could say the "El" of "Elvis", the stadium erupted, and there were a heck of a lot of people. I would love to have been closer, even to have taken field glasses. And to have touched him! I have a friend who used to follow him everywhere. She has all these Elvis scarves and so many tales to tell. I don't understand why people wanted to rip his clothes off when he was on stage, but to have touched him!

His message to the world, was that he was a very simple man, even when he became famous. That was his appeal in Britain. We didn't like snobs. At one stage I liked The Beatles, I still like their music, but the instant they became famous, they went shooting out of Liverpool. He did a lot by his devotion to Memphis.

Jennifer talks of growing to be a stronger Elvis fan as the years have passed, and her interest in his music has also changed. When she was eleven years old, *Jail House Rock* was a favourite, but now it is his spiritual music which she prefers: *If We Never Meet Again This Side of Heaven*, and *Battle of Jericho*. "The spiritual message is this," she says, "have faith in God, whatever your frailties. There is something on the other side. And I don't believe for one instant like all those dirty people say, that he was found reading pornographic books. When he died he was reading about the Turin Shroud. Elvis was searching for his spirituality.

Leslie Stanek

CHANGE OF NAME DEED
BY THIS DEED I, the Undersigned LESLIE STANEK of 54 Pembury Close, Pembury Estate, London E5, DO HEREBY absolutely renounce and abandon the use of my former full name of LESLIE STANEK and in lieu thereof DO ASSUME as from the date hereof the full name of ELVIS ARON PRESLEY

AND IN PURSUANCE OF SUCH CHANGE OF FULL NAME: – I HEREBY DECLARE that I shall at all times hereinafter in all records, deeds and instruments in writing and all actions and proceedings and in all dealings and transactions and on all occasions whatsoever use and sign the said name of ELVIS ARON PRESLEY only

AND I HEREBY AUTHORISE and request all persons to designate and address me by such assumed full name of ELVIS ARON PRESLEY only

IN WITNESS whereof I have hereunto signed my assumed full name of ELVIS ARON PRESLEY and my relinquished Full name of LESLIE STANEK and have set my hand and sealed this 16th day of November 1990.

SIGNED, SEALED and DELIVERED by the above named ELVIS ARON PRESLEY FORMERLY KNOWN AS LESLIE STANEK.

Can an Elvis fan pay any greater homage to the King than to give up his own identity in his honour and adopt the name Elvis Aron Presley? A name is more than one's identity tag. It is not like an official number or identity card, it is part of one's being, character and personality. As a keen student of numerology, Elvis himself certainly believed names contained spiritual and mystical properties. "At the name of Jesus, every knee shall bow," Christians proclaim. A whole school of intellectual inquiry has developed in Judaism around the understanding of the name of God. In Islam, followers are given the name of the Prophet or of one of his close companions as a sign of and guide to faith. In some faiths a new convert is given a new name to mark a moment of transition. Similarly monks and nuns entering a religious order are frequently given a new name, maybe the name of a saint whose example is to be followed in life. A new Pope assumes a new name on election, and followers of Vatican politics often take the choice of name as an indication of how the new pontiff plans to run the church.

It is often thought that the qualities embodied in a name can be passed on to the owner of the name. Thus the daughters of devout Christians have in the past been given such names as Felicity or Grace, and the names have remained in general use. So it is that fans have taken Elvis's name not only to honour Elvis, to give themselves and their own identities over to him, but also to be imbued with his qualities. Leslie, or rather Elvis, is by no means the only person to undergo a name change. There are other Elvises in Britain and probably several hundred Elvis Presleys worldwide.

Ken 'Aaron' Richie

Less dramatic, but more typical, though just as final, was the decision taken by Ken Richie. He and his wife Pam are devoted Elvis fans and from their home in Southampton do all they can to keep a network of other fans in touch with each other and the memory of the King of Rock 'n' Roll. They run *The Official Strictly Elvis Fan Club*, "the club that cares".

Ken changed his name to Aaron when he married Pam in 1983. "There were five Kens in my family, including Kenny, my son. So I took the middle name I had given to the son I had lost four years earlier. He had been called Gene Aaron, Gene after Gene Vincent and Aaron after Elvis Aaron. I am now quite used to being called Aaron. It is unusual but not unheard of, as it comes from the Bible."

While Pam and Aaron have done nothing as drastic as moving to Memphis to live, it would be fair to say they now devote themselves to Elvis. He is their emotional focus and as a couple their relationship appears to be shaped by the presence of this third figure. Indeed they have given up almost all other interests in life to follow him. Their home is full of memorabilia and they organize a range of fund-raising events for charity. They say they are trying, in a small way, to carry on the charity work Elvis did when he was alive. Pam's memories of Elvis go back to 1956.

I remember this peculiar voice coming and going on the transistor radio. I could never quite make out the name as the signal would fade as the DJ said it. It was several weeks before I found out who it was I had been listening to.

The first time I saw his face was on the cover of some sheet music in a music shop. From the first moment I noticed his eyes. Over the years, it is still the eyes I find so fascinating. He would laugh with his eyes and look at you as if you were the most important person in the world. Yet he could also look at you, flash his eyes at you and he would make you feel he knew if you had done something wrong. What I really value is his one to one contact. Elvis has the power to make me feel I am the only one in the room.

Aaron came to know Elvis through his famous comeback television show, made in 1968. It was made when Elvis's popularity was on the wane and presented a whole new Presley to a whole new audience. It was, as some fans now put it, the resurrection of his career. Aaron saw the show in 1969 and says he was "blown away by the image. The leather suit, the movements, the singing all combined. It was just fantastic. From then on I was a dedicated Elvis fan."

For all her adult life Pam has felt an empathy with Elvis. She says he has never let her down. Every important occasion in her life is associated with one of his songs. When he was going through his divorce from Priscilla, Pam and her then husband were also getting divorced. She found comfort in Elvis singing *Always on my Mind*. When she married Aaron in 1983, they arranged a Hawaiian wedding, taking the theme of one of Elvis's best known films. When Elvis died, she says, it took six months for the whole impact of the loss to be fully realised: "I couldn't believe it or accept it. Elvis had always been there. If I had been miserable he had cheered me up. When I was feeling sentimental I would play his quiet romantic music. If I needed to hear something soothing, I would play his religious music."

Aaron was at work when the news reached him and he dropped the coil he was working on at the time. "To get over the worst took me about twelve months, but I do not think I have ever got over the news. Elvis was part of the family. He had always been there. He still is when I need him. I get this feeling that he is there to guide me along. He's a friend, a very close friend."

Pam and Aaron say that life without Elvis would be very dull. Pam cannot travel far for health reasons and Aaron has been unemployed. Elvis, his music and videos, fills their days. To Aaron the religious music is very important. It is to Pam too, but she is quick to dismiss any suggestion that Elvis has been elevated to the status of a God. She quotes Elvis himself, "There is only one King, Jesus." Pam has a prayer written out and hanging on the wall at her home. It is a prayer she says she can imagine Elvis reciting. As to the idea of fans praying to Elvis, Pam is quite accepting. "Why not," she asks, "if they get comfort from it?"

If I felt it would suit me to talk to him in prayer, I probably would. Sometimes I do talk to him. Not a deep conversation, but perhaps if something has happened to do with the fan club, I might turn to one of his pictures and say, "Now look what you've got us into."

Some people say, "But he's dead, why keep remembering

him?" Well, I wouldn't like to die thinking my kids will soon have forgotten me. If that was the case I would have wasted my time living.

Pam and Aaron feel that Elvis brought them together, and brings others together through a mutual interest in his music. "A lot of fans meet through Elvis and later get engaged and marry. This is good because in some couples, one partner likes Elvis, but the other is not too keen. You would be surprised the numbers of husbands who are jealous of Elvis."

*

One classic test of true discipleship is that in which the loyal follower is asked, what are you prepared to give up? Family, money, security? In no formal way does Elvis issue this challenge, but there are without doubt many individuals who have felt such a calling. Some have moved to Memphis to live. Others feel compelled to go on pilgrimage, others to organize clubs and events to perpetuate his memory, or to defend the name and honour of Elvis. Of course in many ways the dedication of these fans is no different to the dedication of the passionate musician, train-spotter, Jason Donovan fan or autograph collector. It is true that the single-minded Elvis fan can be classified alongside all who intensely follow a narrow interest in life. It is a common type of human behaviour. But is there another dimension which puts the Elvis devotee alongside another group? A group which would include the pious Catholic who goes to mass every day and regularly recites the rosary, or the seven day a week Jehovah's Witness door knocker, or the Moonie spending twelve hours a day out in the cold collecting money? A group motivated by a wider spiritual quest . . .

☆

Praying Through Elvis

"You treat him like a God. It's wrong, but you do."

It was after many hours of talking about Elvis and her love for him, that one fan blurted out these words. It was as if she had made a confession, no longer did she have to pretend. Up until that point she had been taking the official line. Fans prayed to God for Elvis, as they would pray for any other dear friend who had died. Then came the admission, "You treat him like a God. It's wrong, but you do."

Many fans truly feel that Elvis was a man with a mission, with a divine purpose. His music has touched so many of them at a spiritual level, they cannot think of him as an ordinary man. In that prayer is the act of spiritual communication, they feel they are justified in praying to or through Elvis. Some will admit to it, others not. Outsiders must take their words and deeds and come to their own conclusions.

Before Ken Welsh, an Elvis impersonator, takes to the stage, as he waits for the dramatic opening and pounding timpany beat of the famous Elvis theme music, *Also Sprach Zarathustra*, he prays to Elvis for strength and guidance.

It is when listening to Elvis's religious music that Linda, a devoted British fan, feels closest to him.

There is an amazing sincerity in his voice. An Elvis fan can feel it. An outsider may not. But if they really sat back and listened. His records bring me nearer to God. I pray to him every night. I pray to God, but I also pray to Elvis, his mum and dad, his twin brother. They are all together and happy together. Elvis, when he lost his mother, was never allowed to grieve. He had to go on and please his fans. He would never let his fans down. That is real respect for his fans and we must show our respect for him.

Linda's friend Marie believes that fans come together to listen to Elvis's music in the way people go to church to pray to God:

I do believe God chose Elvis for a reason on this earth, and I reckon that he did what he wanted him to do and he brought a lot of people nearer to God. That is what the whole thing is about really, getting nearer to God.

Elvis loves all his fans. And I feel that love personally. I feel that a lot of the time he is around. In a sense I talk to him. I talk to him through the music. If I have any problems or feel in any particular mood, I play the appropriate music. If I'm sad, I put on a sad song.

Kiki Apostolakos stresses that Elvis has no divine status. She acknowledges that there are some fans who, in their hearts, feel their hero has greater than mortal status, but she warns against such thinking.

There are many people who think Elvis is a God. But I see it this way. Without God we wouldn't have Elvis. God sends people sometimes to wake us up. To shake us. To ask us, what are we doing, where are we going? Apostle Paul, Apostle Peter, they are not gods, but they were with God.

Without God, we are nothing. If we say Elvis is God and ignore God, we ignore where we come from and where Elvis came from. It is a blasphemy in the face of Elvis. But there are similarities between Elvis and Jesus. They were both betrayed at the end and suffered and both gave out love without asking anything in return. They wanted people to remember them and follow their example. God preached through Jesus. Elvis did not preach but sang.

As David, the musician of the Bible, sang. We have the psalms; maybe Elvis was preaching to the people through his songs.

As Kiki talks of the lives of Elvis and Jesus, tears fill her eyes. She talks of Jesus being born in a stable and of Elvis's humble beginnings in a wooden shack. She talks of Elvis's generosity in life: "Elvis came to prepare us to be closer to God."

A prayer for Elvis appeared in the magazine *Elvis World*. Dated June 1989 it was signed simply, "loving you always. A Friend." It read:

Let me be a link to your happiness and smiles and turn your tears to joy, your sadness to gladness, your pain to love, for I will love you more today than yesterday but less than tomorrow;

Let me fill your lonely hours with caring and let me be a light in your darkness;

Depend on me for each new day to begin, give me your troubles and worries and release them to me for I am with you;

Allow me to be your freedom to be the person you are and want to be, and let me be your ears to hear and listen to you;

Know that we are here for each other, in friendship first, along the unknown path of hopes and dreams, to fill the need in each other to be needed;

Take my hand and trust in me to be the beautiful person I have come to know and love;

Allow the power of faith and belief to strengthen you from day to day and . . . Believe in tomorrow for it will not fail you unless you choose to throw it away, for you are "Always On My Mind" and forever in my heart;

I have so much love to give, let me share it with you and

put love and happiness in your life to replace the tears and
sorrow;
"Thank You" for being the "Very Special Person and Friend"
that you are to me and let this be my "Prayer of Love To
You";
Thank you "for being You."

It is an interesting prayer in that at some points while reading
it one is not sure if it is a prayer by or from Elvis. Some fans
look to Elvis for guidance and protection, others look to offer
Elvis protection themselves. It is almost as if some fans identify
with Gladys and feel Elvis still needs a mother here on earth
to look after his interests. There is, they say, his reputation
and good name to defend against the abusers. It is part, some
fans would say of, to adopt the popular fan motto, "Taking
Care of Elvis."

A fascinating set of theological issues is raised in this
devotional poem from a fan, Eddy Hamilton, of Tyne and
Wear. It was printed in the magazine *Elvisly Yours*. Can God
be blamed and can God be forgiven for what happens on
earth?

> Oh Lord oh God Almighty,
> You took our friend away.
> The effect it had on millions,
> Well, I really could not say.
> Oh God, we do forgive you
> For what you did that day,
> For you are high and mighty
> It's you we all obey.
> But why, God, take him early
> He was only forty-two
> This question we all ask God,
> But the answer lies with you.
> Until such time you call us
> We will never, ever know,
> But we have faith in you God

> We just hope to make it show.
> This prayer I wrote for Elvis
> The words are short and few.
> This is for fans who miss him
> We shall always remember you.

One fan, Mike Challis, writes in his poem as if of a conversion experience:

> Elvis touched my heart
> And my soul began to sing
> I was searching for life's reason,
> And I found the King.
> My mind was lifted higher,
> Way above the earth.
> While deep inside my body
> Love saw its birth . . .
> If there is a heaven,
> And a God whose love is true.
> Then I am sure, Elvis,
> God now lives alongside you.

Some poems written by fans are clearly derived from well-known Christian hymns. Not that there is any intended plagiarism, or even an attempt at pastiche; rather, the hymn format lends itself to the ideas fans wish to express and is clearly, in their minds, associated with spiritual ideas. The use of Christian images and language to express feelings for Elvis is inevitable. They are the most familiar, and in some cases the only images and words available to people raised in the western world. There are for instance many references in tributes and poems by Elvis fans to angels. This is an extract from a poem written by a thirteen-year-old Elvis fan, Adrienne Gardiner from Bristol:

Around you, Angels flocked, Gathered all around,
They sang their praises loudly, To the rock 'n' roll sound.

For centuries, angels, the messengers of heaven, have been associated with special times and holy people. The gospel stories are full of references to angels. In many medieval stories too, angels are associated with special saints. Whenever a story is told which has an allegorical as well as historic dimension, angels, it seems, make an appearance. So it is with Elvis. Two angels flank the statue of Christ which oversees the meditation gardens at Graceland. They are posed in prayer at the feet of Jesus. He stands in front of a cross with his arms stretched out as if blessing the place where Elvis and his family lie. Above the head of Christ are the three letters "IHS", or Jesus, at the base of the statue, in large letters, is written the one word "PRESLEY".

Some fans employ the images and language of the Christian faith to express their feelings about Elvis, while others turn to the language of science fiction. Elvis himself used both sources of imagery when talking about himself and his purpose. He believed in UFOs and read voraciously the esoteric theories which referred back to Atlantis, a brotherhood of masters, and visitors from Venus. As we have seen, his mind was full of Captain Marvel, secret fantasies and exotic ideas. A poem by a London fan entitled *Message from Elvis* talks of "our friends the Milky Way, mysterious in the sky" and ends:

> I know those years on earth
> were really just a trial
> for each to find a mate
> of their eternal style.
> For death is not goodbye
> for we all meet again
> to share eternal youth
> on some Nebula plain.

The rediscovery of Elvis is a theme fans sometimes address. Like a lapsed Christian who rediscovers faith, an Elvis fan who has neglected his or her devotions can return to the family like a prodigal son. *I Met Him Today*, a poem by Paul Brewer, is in this vein:

I found you in amongst all others
With scratches and cracks and dog-eared covers
Your face shone out like a trapped moonbeam
With eyes all starry, as if in a dream.
After wiping the dust from your heavenly sleeve
I placed you on the turntable and then, what relief
Your voice was unhurt and strong as could be
And say "How Great Thou Art" especially for me.

In 1984 Sandra Griffin, a sixteen-year-old from Wiltshire, wrote an unusual fan letter, explaining why she had a special empathy with Elvis. She explained she was a diabetic. "I know what it feels like to be unable to move without having injections, but the King's determination pulled him through."

Elvis has also inspired works of art. One of the best known is the sculpture in downtown Memphis. In Graceland there is a huge portrait of the King which glows with a yellow gold. It is an idealized image comparable to the idealized images of Christ or saints which have been painted over the years. Many amateur artists and Elvis fans produce their own images and icons. They are shown at Elvis meetings, printed in magazines and sometimes sold to raise money for charity. While some of the portraits capture a sadness or pathos, some show Elvis in prayer; none overtly show suffering. The sculptors who have worked on Elvis images normally choose a triumphant image, as if they have caught him striking a pose at the end of *American Trilogy*.

It was only last year that Judy from Mitchell, Illinois, got to stand at the Graceland gate for the first time. She has been a lifelong Elvis fan and first came to love his music when Elvis was still in his youth. But even then she felt Elvis was more than just an entertainer. "He would sing as if he really knew God. That is what opened my eyes when I was a young girl. I was religious also. I felt he had God in his life."

But Judy is an unusual Elvis fan in one respect: she believes Elvis lost contact with God because of his career. Judy cannot entirely dismiss as falsehoods the stories told of his lifestyle towards the end. Yet she remains convinced he was nevertheless basically a good man.

> He believed in God and he is in heaven now. I know he is. God has put him to work in the way that he would want to. Elvis had been put on earth by God to touch people's hearts and minds. Many people came to God through Elvis. His music was very touching to me. He probably led a lot of people to God without even knowing.
>
> When I pray, I pray for Elvis. I know he is in a better place than I am. I know he is safe with God. His death was a tragedy, but he is now where he wants to be with God. So I'm not really sad about his death. I believe in God and Elvis is with him. You probably need to believe in God before you can know Elvis. I think God spoke through Elvis's life.
>
> I don't think there is any reason to pray to Elvis. He is in heaven in a special place like one of the saints. His work here is over.

So do some fans pray to Elvis as if he were a god, or through Elvis, believing he can act as an intercessor, a bridge between them and the world? There are some who are steeped in the ideas Elvis found fascinating, that from time to time, Messiahs or Masters of quasi-divine status walk the earth. They might indeed feel that from somewhere beyond the grave Elvis can intervene in the world's affairs. Many more are probably devoted to Elvis in much the same way that some Christians are devoted to certain saints. In medieval times certain saints became very popular. After his murder, thousands of pilgrims a year visited the tomb of St Thomas à Becket in Canterbury. As a saint it was supposed by many who came to kneel by his earthly remains that he had the ear of God, that they could pray for healing, good fortune or forgiveness to God using St Thomas as the intermediary.

But this form of devotion is not accepted within the Protestant tradition. The preachers from Elvis's Christian background would certainly not have encouraged such practices. So it is that many Elvis fans will hotly deny any suggestion that they have turned their hero into a cult religious figure. In addition to possible Protestant reservations, they sense that for it to be perceived that they have "deified" a popstar will attract unwelcome ridicule. Fans are very sensitive about the way people laugh at the very idea of devotion to a rock and roll singer. Yet, from time to time, a fan will "come out". A volume of poems written by Pam Gale, and described as a "tribute by a devoted fan" contains this verse:

No! we shan't forget you,
Though others say we should,
Your light still shines around us,
And keeps us feeling good.
They say we've made a God of you,
So immortal you've become,
But is it so wrong to admire a man,
For all the good he's done?

☆

FIVE

Do This
in Memory of Me

The long stone wall which fronts Elvis Presley Boulevard and separates the grounds of Graceland from the highway, has for years been the place where fans have left messages for Elvis. As the rain and the passing time clear one set of messages from view, new ones appear. Many are simple expressions of love, but as the years following his death pass by, more and more messages take on a spiritual tone. Some resemble the unpretentious "in memorium" rhymes which often appear in local newspapers to mark the anniversary of the death of "a loved one". Others have style, wit and perceptiveness. Some are so personal they will never be repeated, but others follow an established pattern. These are just a few examples:

"We lost a King, but heaven has gained one."
"Only two people have moved the world so much. Jesus our Lord, and Elvis our King."
"Pray for us and always remember us."
"Elvis, a man before his time who will live for ever."
"We travelled from Germany to be near to you."
"I'm hooked on Elvis. What did I do before I discovered him?"
"Elvis we believe, always and forever."
"Elvis, the world needs you."

"Loving you makes lonely street a lot easier."

"Elvis, if you read this I know you are alive."

"He touched me and now I am no longer the same."

"Elvis, thank you for being our guiding light."

"Every mountain I have had to climb, Elvis carried me over on his back."

"Elvis, your memory lives in every room of my house."

"Mansions in heaven. I see myself walking with the King. The angels are descending to carry me up."

"Wishing, hoping and praying to see Elvis on a paradise earth one day."

"Elvis, I'm having your baby. 29 Sept 91."

"Elvis, you caught me in your trap."

"I saw the ghost of Elvis. He walked up to the gates of Graceland and I saw him walk right through them."

"I heard the call, I made the pilgrimage, I came to Graceland."

"Elvis, I don't care what anyone says, in my heart you live. Thanks for the music."

"Wanted to be here before I died. I made it."

"Hi Elvis, from Stonehenge."

"Fight the power, Elvis was a hero to most."

"Elvis is a God."

"I would like to have known you but I was just a kid and your candle burned out long before."

"Elvis, you always will be the biggest, greatest, the best. Always remembered and cherished. 'Til the next time may God bless you. I love you with all your heart."

"Elvis, thanks to my cousin, your number one fan, I have learned to appreciate the wonderful sounds you made. With all my heart."

"Elvis eternal."

"To the King. I will love you forever. We will meet again soon. Be good."

"Elvis, no matter where you go — there you are."

"Elvis, eternal spirit, blessed by God."

"We planned for eight long years to come pay homage
   to our King,
Inspite of all the barriers we were determined our love
   to you we'd bring.
When we finally stood outside Graceland door,
The sacrifices we had made, we would make again
   and more.
To see the home that you had made,
To walk the paths where once you trod.
We only wish that you were here,
Instead of at the hand of God."

"Elvis, from one of your newest fans, take care of all of
us."
"Thanks for making our honeymoon so special."
"Elvis the values you tried to hold on to shall live on."
"In memory of our Mum and Dad."
"Elvis, we believe always and forever."
"Elvis, your spirit lit my way, I hope to see you again."
"Elvis your music fills the room of my house every moment
of the day. I wake up to your beautiful voice."
"Elvis, I still feel you're here."
"Elvis we're having your baby, we love you."
"Elvis I keep coming to see you. When are you coming back.
I know you are still alive."

       Coming back from Lubbock,
       I thought I saw Jesus on the plane,
       But it might have been Elvis,
       They look kinda the same.

"Elvis is undead."

The messages cover every aspect of Elvisdom. Every day there
are new fans with felt pens arriving to make their mark. And,
inevitably, in and amongst the messages from the faithful, a
few wags have left their contributions:

"Elvis, you came, you saw, you conquered, you croaked."

"Elvis, can I please use your bathroom?"

"Cut the rot Elvis, we know you're alive. So get back here as soon as you can so that you can clean this damn wall."

Graceland draws nearly 700,000 visitors a year. It was built in neo-classical style on a 13.8 acre site in 1939 by a Memphis physician, Dr Thomas Moore, who named it after an aunt. In November 1991, the city's most famous house at 3764 Elvis Presley Boulevard was officially placed on the register of Historic Places. It joined 1,100 other national sites identified with major American figures. Graceland won its place alongside the homes of many famous American presidents, as a result of a submission prepared by a twenty-two-year-old student, who visited Graceland and was surprised to find it had no national historic plaque on view. Graceland was opened to the public as a museum and memorial five years after Elvis died. It is now said to attract more visitors than any house in the USA except the White House in Washington DC.

The peak month for visitors is July, the main American vacation month, followed by August. During the summer between 2,000 and 5,000 visitors come to Graceland every day. Steve Marshall works for the Presley estate at Graceland dealing with public relations:

For the most part visitors are just everyday people. Everyone is an Elvis fan to a certain extent, but they are not particularly big fans. They come out of curiosity. They are in the area and say, let's go and see Elvis's house. Five per cent of the visitors who come, especially in Elvis week in August, are the dedicated Elvis fans. Most of them are very nice and wonderful people. They are really into Elvis.

During August they'll tour the house every day as well as go to all the other events and attend the vigil. It is a growing event. This year we had about 35,000 to 40,000 people that came during that week. In 1992, we are expecting 60,000 people. Elvis's fandom is growing by leaps and bounds. In

Britain I believe there is the largest Elvis Presley club in the world, boasting over 20,000 members. Just because Elvis physically died, his music and his talent didn't.

To celebrate Elvis's birthday in January, fans meet outside the mansion and sing Happy Birthday. A proclamation is read and representatives of the city of Memphis are present. Across the street a cake is then ceremonially cut. But the major gathering is in the summer around the time of the anniversary of Elvis Presley's death. Graceland is then the focus of a huge pilgrimage. There is no exact count of the numbers of fans who arrive, but it must be many tens of thousands. The climax of the week is the candlelight vigil, which, all observers agree, grows in size year by year. It begins with a brief opening ceremony at the gates produced by the *Elvis Country Fan Club*. These eye-witness accounts and brief impressions from fans, family and Graceland staff give just some idea of the occasion.

We start at nine o'clock on the fifteenth and wait for the guard to get a light from the eternal flame at the graveside. We then light a candle from the torch and at ten o'clock start a procession to the grave, to lay a flower and stand a moment and meditate. And we walk around slowly. It can last until three in the morning. As I stand at his graveside I thank him for being Elvis, for giving me the music and for making me really happy, because I can't imagine life without Elvis or his music.

They play Elvis music, beautiful music and it is almost like a religious experience.

You feel the emotion through your bones. You can hardly see Elvis's grave it is so full of flowers. I feel as if it is Good Friday. To me it is another Good Friday in the year. These are the words of Kiki who visits Elvis's grave every other day of the year. "On the anniversary, I think about the suffering. I think of why they put him on the cross. Even from his cross Jesus was saying, forgive them. He did nothing bad. The same with Elvis. Just before he died there was a book to be published saying so many unpleasant things about Elvis. Why did they attack him? One or two of them were like Judas. Sometime they will have to face God and how they will face Elvis up there, I don't know."

Harold Loyd, Elvis's cousin, is one of the torch bearers.

We light our torches off the eternal flame by Elvis's grave and march down to the gate and stand on each side and the fans light their candles and walk in single file up to the grave and circle it. It is beautiful but sad. We see a lot of people in tears.

A fan who attended the fifth anniversary candlelit procession talked of lasting memories and the beauty of the event:

Thousands of fans had gathered outside Graceland leading up to midnight. For the first time ever . . . fans were allowed up to the graveside at midnight . . . It had been raining all day, much of the time torrentially. As if decreed by God the rain miraculously stopped just before midnight. Every person held a candle . . . except one little boy . . . fast asleep in his father's arms. His family had come all the way from South America.

The thousands who arrive for the candlelit procession inevitably cause a considerable organisational headache. If the slow line falters, or there is a blockage at the gate, it is has been known for some fans to faint in the crush. They have a similar problem at the world's greatest place of pilgrimage, Mecca. But do Elvis fans feel obliged to visit Graceland in the way that a Muslim is obliged to go on Haj, pilgrimage, to Mecca? Obviously there is no formal requirement as there is in Islam, but echoes of the Islamic obligation are to be found. This call comes from an editorial in an edition of *Elvisly Yours*: "You MUST visit

Graceland, this year, next year, or in your lifetime – just to see what this man achieved."

*

On an ordinary day Graceland is busy from morning through to dusk. Every few minutes visitors stop their cars in the lay-by alongside the front wall and briefly get out to write a message on the stonework or pose for a photograph by the famous gate with its metalwork design depicting musical notes. Across the road even more people gather – the visitors who have come not for a brief stop of homage, but to spend the day at Graceland and visit the mansion, museum and grounds. They have parked their cars on the carpark behind the huge private jet now sited opposite the house. It is Elvis's private plane, which he named "Lisa Marie", after his daughter. For a fee Elvis fans can take a look inside. The smaller plane, the Jetstar "Hound Dog 2" stands alongside. They can also visit the automobile museum, which has Elvis Presley's unmistakable pink Cadillac mounted on a stand outside. Some fans will recognize the middle-aged gentleman in uniform who takes their tickets as Harold Loyd, Elvis's first cousin. Inside they will see twenty of the star's personal cars, motorbikes and motorized toys, including his flashy Stutz Blackhawk, as well as his gas credit card and driving licence. They can also visit a number of souvenir shops and a movie theatre as well as the reception centre where tickets are sold for tours of the mansion, grounds and trophy room. The 1991 price was adults $7.95 and children $4.75.

The tours are highly organized. Every few minutes a small busload of fans drive across the highway and up the drive to the mansion. There parties of a couple of a dozen at a time are shepherded through selected rooms. Only five of the twenty-three rooms are open to view in the mansion house. The guides explain that the upstairs living quarters are out of bounds. Even they, the employees, are not allowed into the holy of holies. Elvis's aunt still lives in the house and only she and a few select visitors are allowed to see where Elvis slept and died. The few privileged people who have been up the stairs say little has changed since the day Elvis's body was found there. His clothes are there as are many of his personal effects. Fans believe it is kept as a time-capsule of the day Elvis died. Steve Marshall does not believe the whole house will ever be opened up to the fans. "Structurally it would be difficult. But the main reason is that when Elvis was at Graceland the upstairs was his retreat and the family have requested it stay that way. I cannot see them changing their mind."

Steve is one of the very few employees to have been allowed up to Elvis's private area. "It is strange, it is frozen in time. To go there makes you aware that Elvis was a real person. He had sock drawers and a closet. He was a human being and lived like everyone else. It's not spooky, you get more of a warm feeling. It is very nice. It was a privilege to go."

Fans are, however, shown the dining room, the pool room, with its ornate curtain drape decor, and a bizarre room called the African, or Jungle Room, filled with strangely carved wooden furniture. Vernon's office is also preserved and looks curiously dated, as does Elvis's television room where he watched a variety of channels simultaneously. A collection of Elvis's gold and platinum discs is on display in the purpose built Trophy Room as well as some of his most famous costumes, awards, portraits and guns. He was fond of guns, firing them at targets for fun or television sets in anger.

Like pilgrims to the Holy Land who walk alongside the Sea of Galilee and tread the streets of Jerusalem to follow the path of Jesus, many fans thrill at the thought that they are walking in the footsteps of Elvis. So would Elvis fans like greater access to the house? Some undoubtedly would, but Jennifer Walker, who makes frequent visits to Graceland since moving to Memphis, speaks for the fans who want the mystique to remain. "I am not a personal friend of Elvis's family and I feel I would be infringing on his privacy. The family have said they wish the house to be as it was, and when Elvis was alive, he had his own private areas." Is she being careful to do nothing that might risk shattering an illusion? Can one still idolize a super hero when you've seen the bathroom where he ignominiously collapsed and died?

As is common with many public buildings in the USA, Graceland is well used to assisting visitors with disabilities. Although the basement rooms are out of bounds to wheelchair users, because of the steep stairs, every other part of the house and estate is accessible. Indeed Graceland, like many religious shrines and places of pilgrimage, attracts a high number of visitors with disabilities. One of the regular causes for which the British *Strictly Elvis* fan club raises money is to send "handicapped fans" to Graceland. When a party of people with disabilities arrives, Graceland can almost resemble that other famous place of pilgrimage, Lourdes. What motivates fans to raise money for the specific purpose of sending a disabled fan to Graceland? Lying behind it all, is there an unspoken thought that somehow the atmosphere and associations of Graceland might have healing or restorative powers? Physical miracles are not necessarily expected, the healing can take the form of giving the fan new purpose and hope – although healings, through or by Elvis, have been reported.

*

One of the first British visitors to be shown around at the time of its official opening was Sid Shaw, the Elvis fan who has turned his fascination with Elvis into a business, marketing souvenirs of the star. He calls Graceland the eighth wonder of the world! He described entering the house between the two stone lions and the huge classic columns which guard the front door:

I was walking through the same doorway Elvis walked through for all those years. Inside the entrance hall conjures up images of Victoriana or Vienna opera houses. Everywhere, right, left, front behind, on the floor is red, very vivid red. You sink into the thickest red carpet ever imagined. You could fall from anywhere in Graceland and not get hurt, so thick is the carpet.

Sid then described the dining room with glass everywhere, and the living room, and what he called a strange room, "just curtains and completely bare and totally enclosed except for a grand piano and one chair – the Music Room. It was like a mother's womb. Of course the curtains were deep red."

The place, however, every fan sets his or her heart on visiting is the grave. There flanked by the graves of his father, mother, grandmother and a memorial to his stillborn twin, lies Elvis Aaron Presley. Overlooking the family is a huge stone image of Christ which carries the one word, Presley. There are always fresh bouquets of flowers on and around the grave and cards and letters from fans. At the head of the grave there is a design bearing the initial letters of the Elvis motto, "Taking Care of Business" and the lightning flash symbol. Beneath it burns an eternal flame.

At Christmas, Graceland is ablaze with lights and a huge Christmas crib is built on the front lawn. In his life Elvis always stipulated that Graceland had to be dressed at its best for the twenty-fifth of December.

*

Elvis's birthplace at Old Saltillo Road (now Elvis Presley Drive) in Tupelo has been restored and is also open to the public. The tiny two-roomed wooden shack-house is simply furnished with furniture of the time that Elvis was born there. The house was built by Vernon with timber for which he had to pay a borrowed $180. It was restored in 1977 by local volunteers and is preserved as a Mississippi historical site in a basic idealised form. One gets little feel of the grinding poverty of the inter-war American depression. There are no chickens running around and no cow out the back as there would have been when Elvis was small. However, to followers it is like a sacred place and visitors enter and leave with a hushed reverence. In front of the house is a small plaque which reads, "BIRTHPLACE OF ELVIS PRESLEY. Elvis Aaron Presley was born Jan 8, 1935 in this house, built by his father. Presley's career as a singer and entertainer redefined American popular music. He died Aug 16, 1977 at Memphis, Tennessee."

Behind the house is the Elvis Presley Centre which also doubles as a community hall. It hosts wedding receptions, parties and reunions. The land around Elvis's house is now owned by the town, having been bought with money given by Elvis Presley raised at a concert in the town, and is a recreation area for the townsfolk. The shop at the visitor's centre sells souvenirs, including small squares of cloth cut from clothes Elvis once owned, perhaps even wore. Tupelo has none of the garishness of Graceland and is looked after by local people through the Tupelo based Elvis Presley Commission, rather than employees of a multi-million dollar memorabilia business. The commission was set up in August 1977 and given the responsibility of "overseeing and governing the use of the birthplace, youth centre and attendant facilites".

The third building on the site is the Elvis chapel. The Elvis chapel is a complete surprise by comparison with the other places of pilgrimage. Of Elvis's possessions only his Bible is on show. It is a small tasteful Christian place of worship with a striking modern stained glass window covering one wall. It is not dedicated to Elvis worship in any way, rather dedicated to his memory, in the way that a church might be dedicated to a saint. No regular services are held there, but it is used for weddings when Elvis fans are looking for a suitable place to marry. According to the official literature, "In August 1979, countless hours of planning, dreaming and praying bore fruit when the magnificent Elvis Presley Memorial Chapel was dedicated. It stands as a lasting monument to Elvis's fans and friends around the world because it was financed entirely from their donations with administration by the Elvis Presley Commission."

Some people look at the symbolism incorporated in the main window of the chapel and detect a more enigmatic message than one would assume from first glancing at the neutral abstract design. There appears to be a cross and a dove and a hand reaching down. Is it the hand of God, some wonder, or that of Elvis reaching down from his heavenly stage? And what of the design which could be taken for a crown. A crown is worn by a King. Is it that of Christ or Elvis? And what should the fan make of the pattern of interlocking rings. Was not Elvis the giver of rings at his concerts? And what of the overall impression of the window: is it designed to give some impression of the dazzling costumes Elvis wore?

One of the team running the shop and Elvis centre is Diane Brown:

At first the house was only open by appointment. Then we kept it open through the week and now it is all the year round except Thanksgiving Day and Christmas Day. August is the busiest month because so many fans come to Graceland on the anniversary of his death and make the trip to Tupelo as well. A lot of fans also come in January on his birthday. They come from all over the world.

The chapel is peaceful and quiet and was built by his friends. Some of the fans spend a long time there. It is a good place to sit down and meditate and collect your thoughts. It was intended that the chapel would be a special place to pray. That is the spirit in which fans come here. He had himself said that he would like one day to see a little meditation garden or chapel here in the park in Tupelo, so that when fans visited his house they could visit a place of prayer. That was the inspiration for it. The fans made it a reality.

When some fans arrive at his birthplace, they just burst into tears with emotion. It is kind of amazing to me that they are still so touched after all these years. But many come in happy mood with stories to tell of when they saw him in concert, or met him. For some, they admit, it has been a lifelong ambition to come to Tupelo and are amazed they have finally made it.

I know that Elvis is dead, but I wouldn't disagree with fans who come to a place like this and say they still feel him very much alive in spirit. Some people perhaps go too far.

There are people, as with any great public person, who carry things to extremes and focus too much on the one individual. I have seen people come here who are fanatical. They are fanatics, not fans. They are obsessed.

I hope they don't go into the chapel to pray to Elvis. That was not the intention. That is not the spirit of the place.

Fanatics or fans, the common reaction of visitors to the little house is one of awe. They are surprised at how simple were the megastar's beginnings. Kim Stokes is one of the younger team working at the Tupelo birthplace area. She was only eight years old when Elvis died, but she "grew up with Elvis" and vividly recalls the day of his death and the shock waves that went through the community. Today she regularly witnesses the awestruck expressions of visitors who arrive to see his old home.

They see just two rooms, the kitchen area and the bedroom. There was no electricity and there was no indoor toilet. They barely had money to put food on the table. When Elvis was here for the first two and a half years of his life it was just a very poor area of town. It was during the depression years.

The fans are really humbled by the place. He came from nowhere and talent got him to where he went.

A true fan will search out five other key sites in Tupelo as well as those associated with his birth. There is the Assembly of God Church where the Presley family attended Sunday worship. It is located on Adam Street and is now known as the East Heights Assembly of God Church. Two of the schools Elvis attended can also be seen. He attended Lawhon School up to fifth grade, and was there when he entered a local talent competition and won second place singing *Old Shep*. Milam Junior High School is where the older Elvis was again a rather undistinguished student until, in the eighth grade, he left and moved with his parents to Memphis. The other two sites pointed out are the Tupelo Hardware store where Elvis bought his first guitar and the fairground, to where, as a famous entertainer, he returned to give concerts.

*

Back up the freeway to Memphis, fans with an extra day or two to spare can also search out the sites in downtown Memphis associated with the star. The Sun Recording Studio at 706 Union Avenue is now designated a city landmark because of its legendary associations with the young Elvis. It was here in the summer of 1953 that he recorded his first two tracks, *My Happiness* and *That's When your Heartache Begins*. The American Sound Studios, where Elvis held recording sessions in 1969, can also be seen. Amongst the thirty-five numbers immortalised at American Sound were *In the Ghetto* and *Suspicious Minds*. Fans with a good city map and a true sense of dedication and exploration can find scores of places associated with Elvis, ranging from Humes High School, where he was a pupil, to the Mid South Hospital where he had a face lift in 1975, to the company on Highway 70 which serviced the Graceland swimming pool for Elvis.

The focus of attention and devotion to a true fan is however always the meditation garden where Elvis, his twin brother, his father, mother and grandmother are all remembered. The bodies of all, bar Jesse Garon, his twin, who lies in an unmarked grave in Priceville Cemetery in Tupelo, are said to be there beneath the Tennessee soil. In the summer, fans are given ninety minutes a day to visit the meditation garden without being hassled by the tour parties and without being charged an entry fee. They can spend between 6 and 7.30 am at the graveside. During the Elvis week a two hour evening period is allowed, when the Presley grave plot is often surrounded by devotees standing in quiet tribute, some with tears in their eyes.

But "what is one to meditate upon in this garden?" asks the writer Sue Bridwell Beckham. "Traditionally a place for meditation has been associated with a particular religion. More recently it has been fashionable to build non-sectarian sites for contemplation on university campuses and in public parks. But at Graceland the presence of the Presley family graves seems to suggest that the visitor is to meditate not on a religious symbol of choice but rather on the holiness of the Presleys. That the fans see it this way is testified to by the fact that the garden and the graves are always decorated with floral contributions from visiting fans."

To the loyal fans, those who visit the Presley graves over and over again, the meditation garden is a place of peace and tranquillity and love. Recalling the many times she has stood there by the grave, thinking about the old days when Elvis was alive, Jennifer Walker admits, "in a sense, you almost feel he is looking down from above and thinking, 'oh, I like this'. Automatically I blow a kiss to the heavens and make the sign of the cross. In the years I have lived here in Whitehaven in Memphis, I have never passed Graceland once without making the sign of the cross and blowing a kiss. Spiritually, he's there."

SIX

Icons and Relics

There is nothing new in the sale of relics. For centuries pilgrims have treasured sacred souvenirs of the one they have travelled to venerate. Chaucer mocked the medieval scoundrels who preyed on the gullibility of the faithful who travelled to Canterbury to pray at the grave of Thomas the Martyr. They sold stones and pigs bones to the unwary, pretending they were the remains of holy people or holy places. In *Canterbury Tales* he said of one notorious vendor of pious false merchandise:

> He hadde a croys of latoun, ful of stones,
> And in a glas he hadde pigges bones.
> But with these relikes, whan that he fond
> A povre person dwelling up-on land,
> Up-on a day he gat him more moneye
> Than that the person at in monthes tweye.
> And thus, with feyned flaterye and japes,
> He made the person and the people his apes.

While there is a trade between fans in such items as scarves and shirts as worn by the King, in the main the souvenirs sold make no claims to have been the personal property of the man they honour. Some more closely resemble icons. They are idealised pictures of Elvis in certain familiar poses. Some show him striking the rebellious postures of his youth, but most show him as the clean-cut all-American youth, the Elvis of the films. A few show him in prayer. Many are destined for pride of place in a personal collection of such pictures, a kind of shrine in an individual fan's home.

In addition there are bracelets and necklaces often carrying the letters TLC or TCB; they function not just as decoration, but as a sign of belonging to the international Elvis "family" of fans and as a talisman. One fan recalls how desperate she felt in hospital on one occasion when she was asked to remove her TLC necklace. She felt as if she were abandoning the protection of Elvis.

When Elvis was alive, Colonel Parker ensured there was a good supply of cheap souvenirs of "his boy" for the fans to buy. One of the big criticisms of Colonel Parker was that there was too much of the fairground hustler in him and too little of the big-time strategist. He was so interested in looking at how to hawk the maximum quantity of knick-knacks, that he failed to see Elvis's mega-potential on the international scene.

When Elvis died, however, while the market for the mass-produced items continued, a new interest developed. There was a demand for relics. Anything, for which it could be claimed, a personal association with the King. When the crowds continued to gather outside Graceland for days and weeks after Elvis's death was announced, many fans wanted relics of the King to take with them. Some began to pick stones off the wall. To divert them from this, Harold Loyd hit on the idea of collecting fallen leaves and twigs and handing them out:

One night I was running my legs off picking up leaves for them and sometimes breaking off low hanging limbs from the trees. As I started walking up the drive I kept breaking off more limbs, and when I got my arms full I went back to the gates and opened the gates. As I walked out to them I told them I had enough for everyone if they would divide them up. Just as I got about two feet from them, this lady reached out and grabbed all the limbs from my arms. The others began grabbing them from her and she was screaming at them to "Stop, stop, stop!" I guess she got mad. She screamed at them to keep their damn hands off but they weren't listening to her. I was shocked and maybe a little scared at what was happening. I got back inside the gates fast and shut them in a hurry. I told them they must be crazy. I said I wasn't going to get any more leaves for anybody. After an hour or so, I did get some more leaves and threw them over the gates. I sure wasn't going to be the cat that fell into the yard with the dogs. I love my hair too much for that, and my life too, I might add.

Harold, perhaps more than anyone else, has watched the fans and observed their devotion and loyalty. He has seen, since Elvis's death, an ever increasing demand for souvenirs from inside the Graceland wall. "I guess I can understand it a lot better now. They feel like if it comes from inside, it is closer to him and makes them feel that they have a part of him to hold on to."

So it is, for instance, that one of the thousands of leaves taken from Graceland is now carefully preserved in a flat in Southampton. There, amongst all their pictures and other mementoes, is the inconspicuous dried leaf, which to Aaron and Pam Richie is a treasured link with the home of their idol.

The souvenir shops in and around Graceland are full of standard wares, adapted in the factories where they are made for sale to Elvis fans. Little teddy bears in china with huge red hearts, no doubt made for a general mass market, have "I love Elvis" messages stuck on as an afterthought. Similarly the mugs, thimbles, pens, T-shirts are from standard production lines with modifications to turn them into Elvis merchandise. These things are bought by visitors who come to Memphis as general sightseers. The true fans who travel to pay homage to the King also buy these souvenirs as icons but value the relics infinitely more. They trade relics amongst themselves and go to specialist dealers who can supply them with the more meaningful items. Leaves and twigs from Graceland are, inevitably, quite common. Real importance is attached to objects known to have been touched by Elvis. When Elvis was alive he frequently handed out rings and scarves to his fans from the stage during performances. The rings were inexpensive and worn briefly and designed to be given away. Similarly the scarves were only worn momentarily and one of Elvis's entourage would be at hand with a supply of them for Elvis to quickly put around his neck and then give away to one of the outstretched hands in front of him. These are the treasured items now that Elvis is no longer available to give concerts.

From time to time a more valuable "relic" comes up for sale. Elvis sometimes handed out objects of greater value than the cheap rings and scarves he always had to hand. In 1974 he was singing to a crowd of 8,000 screaming fans when he spotted a five-year-old girl in the audience. He invited her on stage and sang a song specially for her. He then placed a scarf around her neck. But the magic of the day was shattered a short while later when an aggressive older fan snatched the scarf from the little girl and made off with it. Elvis saw what happened and came to the rescue. He took a gold chain necklace with a cross pendant from around his neck and gave it to the child. "This is yours, baby, and nobody can take it away from you." That is until the little girl grew up to be a woman herself and a mother. Times were hard and she desperately needed money. So she put the necklace up for sale.

Even items which Elvis never personally owned can fetch high prices if they can claim an "antique" value. D J Fontana, the drummer who backed Elvis during nearly fifty recording sessions between 1958 and 1964, remembers occasions going to see Elvis in the fifties when "there were Hound Dog hats and Elvis lipsticks everywhere you turned. We would kick them aside to make room to walk and sit. We could have taken what we wanted then, but we didn't. Now I see some of that Elvis lipstick from those days selling for $1000."

When a major item of Elvisana comes on the market, it can

fetch thousands of pounds. In the mid-eighties Sotheby's, the leading auctioneers, held a sale of Elvis memorabilia. One item which attracted particular attention was a black suede jacket worn by Elvis in concert in 1969. Accompanied by two letters of authentification, one from Larry Geller and another from Joe Esposito, it was described in the pre-sale catalogue as "hand made with wide standing collar, seams stuck down,the whole edged with scarlet thongs crudely stitched and forming three ties for fastening. The collar bearing signs of wear." When the auctioneer's hammer finally fell, it was sold for £4,500 to the Hard Rock Cafe, benefiting the Variety Club Sunshine Appeal. With the money raised at the auction a minibus, named the Elvisly Yours Sunshine Coach, was bought for and presented to a South London school. Sotheby's also sold a rare Elvis autograph note for $13,200. It was found crumbled and discarded by Elvis in a Las Vegas hotel room wastepaper basket. It reads: "I feel so alone sometimes. The night is quiet for me. I would love to be able to sleep. I have no need for all this. Help me Lord."

The most valuable and important items are of course to be seen in the Elvis museums. The biggest and best is inevitably at Graceland and archivists are still working on the items which are not on display. In addition, the Elvis impersonator Gary Wayne Bridges tours with his own Elvis Presley Museum, which includes not only such more obvious items as guitars, costumes and cars, but also Elvis Presley's razor and shaving kit!

Also on public display is an object described as a wart or cyst surgically removed from Elvis in life and now preserved in a phial. And more than one million fans, so it has been claimed, have seen travelling exhibits in Canada and the USA at shopping malls and other places where a steady stream of visitors can be guaranteed.

In Sweden an Elvis museum has been set up and in the south east of England an Elvis impersonator travels from market to market with his peripatetic Elvis shop.

The postcards and posters the Elvis fans buy also tell a story. The tourists may send home a few "I've been to Graceland" messages; the fans prefer the pictures of Elvis in prayer or the one which looks as if the spirit of Elvis is walking on the waters of the river Mississippi. Postcards of the meditation gardens where the "holy family" rests are also popular.

In her study of Elvis shrines and souvenirs Sue Bridwell Beckham writes, "If the ambivalent purpose of the meditation gardens suggests that Elvis Presley is accorded near-divinity, the Christmas cards sold at Graceland offer even more. Any who doubt that Elvis followers make some kind of confused association between Elvis and the founder of the Christian religion need only contemplate the reasons for making Christmas greetings cards out of the images of an Elvis shrine." Christmas Day is only two weeks before Elvis's birthday, both are mid-winter festivals. Sue Bridwell Beckham continues,

> Traditional Christmas cards feature images of the birthplace of Jesus, visitors to his birthplace (shepherds, magi) or symbols used in the Christian church (candles, bibles, flowers) – the holiday is, after all, supposed to be a celebration of Jesus's birthday. Even secular Christmas cards made use of traditional symbols – holly, reindeers, snow scenes. Occasionally in the United States at least, greeters will send pictures of their own families and homes or institutional cards with pictures of the main building of the institution. But one suspects that the Graceland Christmas cards are unique in suggesting that people send greetings with images of the home of a popular cult hero. Whether these cards are supposed to suggest shared grief at the loss of Elvis, one-upmanship in that the sender is more devoted than the receiver, or the fact that Elvis is one with the other symbols appropriate to a religious holiday is unclear. It is clear, however, that these cards sell and, presumably, are sent.

In due course fans in the USA hoped that they would be able to send their postcards and Christmas cards through the mail bearing Elvis stamps. Despite fierce lobbying, the Postmaster

General resisted the idea of celebrating Elvis in this way, but in the end the fans had their way. The image to be shown on the stamp is a youthful Elvis singing into an old fifties microphone. It was the fans' choice.

Some people might accuse the Presley estate business managers, who are taking care of business until Lisa Presley comes into her inheritance, of keeping the Elvis cult alive by clever manipulative marketing. To this accusation the estate's public relations spokesman, Steve Marshall, has a ready answer:

It would take a really deliberate effort to mess this Elvis thing up. Elvis was so dynamic, he sells himself. He has such a tremendous following and had such a tremendous talent, there is no marketing to it. It is phenomenon and the reason why people still care is because Elvis represented the American dream to its fullest extent. He went from humble beginnings to being the world's greatest entertainer; he is such an icon that he will always be in people's conscious. He intrigues people even outside America as the American dream is now the international dream. Everyone dreams of making themselves just a little bit better. Europeans and Asians and all the people in the world can identify with Elvis. They want to achieve the things Elvis achieved and he is their symbol of that.

Everybody loves their stars and Elvis Presley is the ultimate star. At the end things went wrong for Elvis. That is the tragedy of the world. Everyone has problems and failures and Elvis was no saint. He was a human being, not a God. And such a lot of pressure was put on him and the human being is not made to be able to deal with such pressure, that fame and that fortune that quick.

As well as the managers of the Presley estate, there are others who have made Elvis their business. These were just some of the hundreds of items for sale by mail order in the magazine *Elvisly Yours*, number 40:

Satin replica autograph scarf – £2.95
Plastic Elvis Presley Boulevard street sign – £1.95
Set of three "Elvis Lives On" clothes patches – £1.95
Elvis soap and soap dish in gift box – £3.95
Candy dish with full colour Elvis portrait – £2.50
Rare imported colour photo sets "for the real collector or the lady who just likes to drool" – any five sets from £10
Picture discs, The gospel songs, *Teddy Bear* or any of the six others – £5.95
Replica TCB gold-plated ring – £8.95
Authentic replica Elvis sunglasses – £7.95
Full colour posters, Army, kung fu, 1955 Tupelo concert – £4.50
The Complete Elvis song book – £12.95
Elvis Thimble – £1.95

And amongst the records available, *His Hand in Mine* at £9.95, the first ever Russian Elvis Album at £7.95 and the Elvis Interviews at £9.95.

It is an undeniable sign of demand for a product when the counterfeiters move in. Bootleg recordings of Elvis's shows and of rare film have plagued the "official" Elvis merchants from the early days. When in 1983, Joe Esposito, a long serving member of the Elvis inner circle, came to Britain, he showed some rare 8mm home movies of Elvis. Fans immediately asked if copies were available. But so as to avoid the danger of having the first few videos sold and then copied, it was stipulated by the distributors that only if 1,000 fans paid £1 up front for the £30, hour long video, would it be made available. During his life, Elvis gave so many live performances and recorded so much unreleased material in studios, that dozens of bootleg recordings were made and sold. Today some of the best are much sought after by fans, who, once they have a complete set of official recordings, often turn to collecting the unofficial recordings to make sure they have as complete a record of Elvis as possible. There is an interesting parallel in the sale of papal souvenirs when the Pope is on tour. In some countries, when the devout arrive to hear and see Pope John Paul, they are often warned not to buy souvenirs from the unofficial touts at the entrance to the venue. These warnings from the local church are made for no other reason than the fact that authorized sales staff inside the stadium, offering similar wares, have been licenced by the church, and pay a percentage to the church for the privilege of hawking their souvenir programmes and photographs of the Pope inside.

The sale of Elvis wares has raised questions in the minds of some fans who wonder if the Elvis legacy is not being exploited commercially. Money is undoubtably made from the business, but the profits, apart from those made by the Presley estate and which will in due course be inherited by Lisa Presley, are not huge. In the main, Elvis fans are not wealthy people. Nevertheless, the Elvis estate tries to keep a tight rein on who uses the image of the King on merchandise. There have been long and acrimonious court battles to sort out who does and who does not have the right to sell Elvis souvenirs.

Accusations of commercialism lie behind some of the main disputes in Elvisdom. The *Elvisly Yours* fan club is run by a man, Sid Shaw, who has a major business selling pop souvenirs. He has been criticized for this supposed conflict of interest and loyalty. Yet he is also an Elvis fan, and his supporters would argue strongly that he has merely turned his passion in life into his livelihood. Who, they say, complains that ministers of religion get a salary, or that some Christians run religious book shops? These fans tell a parable of the Elvis fan who met a man selling photographs of the King. He rebuked him for profiting from Elvis. The man explained that he needed to make a profit on each item sold in order to feed his children. The fan was not satisfied and complained loudly to his friends, saying they should not buy from this dealer. A little while later, the fan wanted a picture of Elvis for his house. When he met the trader again he asked if he could buy one from him. But because business had been so bad as a result of being boycotted, the trader had switched to selling football scarves, and so the fan had to go without the Elvis picture he wanted.

It seems there are few purists amongst the Elvis fans. Trade at the Graceland souvenir shops is brisk. Mail order catalogues are still sent out. Treasured relics are still traded between devotees, although a fan normally needs a very good reason to part with a truly special item. Trade can sometimes be slow in times of recession. But in the foreseeable future souvenir items at the lower end of the market will continue to be bought and sold; if only because so many are so shoddily made, they have to be replaced at regular intervals.

☆

The Priesthood

Can a religion be complete without a priesthood? Of course, and many great faiths have no special caste of those ordained and inititated into exclusive rites and duties.

Or to try another question, if a cult or an organisation which has a spiritual dimension or purpose appears to have a priesthood, does that make it a religion? It is certainly an additional factor in arriving at such a classification, for it is hard to see how a priesthood can be sustained or even exist without a religion. For a priestly order needs a purpose, it needs a creed to serve and a system of belief from which it derives its authority.

Can it be argued that the Elvis cult has a priesthood? Yes, though it is not a formal priesthood with established practices of apprenticeship, training and initiation. But that is only because the cult is so new. The priesthood exists as a body of men, or at least almost exclusively men, who dress in a style of clothing which can be compared to vestments. They perform certain actions to bring the devotees closer to the one they adore, to be a perpetual memory of the man from whom they are separated and in their own bodies they represent that man and that memory to the people when they gather for that purpose. These Elvis "priests" talk of their role, of their calling, as Christian priests talk of theirs. They talk of their love for Elvis and their devotion to his service. Yet they would not think in terms of themselves being akin to a priesthood. They borrow many Christian phrases and ideas to express their thoughts, but to acknowledge to themselves or others that they have a priestly vocation would not come naturally. This may be because the Christian language adopted by many Elvis followers is drawn from the American Protestant tradition which does not itself warm to the ideas of priesthood familiar in the Catholic traditions. They rather talk of allowing themselves the privilege of paying tribute to Elvis in their actions and of preserving his memory: they are the Elvis impersonators.

One image of Elvis himself in performance was of the great high priest. His highly decorated costumes bore many similarities to the vestments of the priest presiding at the Catholic mass. Had he been standing behind an altar, his high collars and the spectacular designs on his white jumpsuits could have been mistaken for the garb of a priest celebrating the eucharist. He was announced on stage by the music of Richard Strauss which was composed to stimulate in the imagination of the listener the awe and majesty of the ancient middle-eastern Zoroastrian priesthood. There is a passage from a more familiar scripture which here needs a mention. In Exodus Chapter 28, the Bible tells of the founding of the old Jewish priesthood by Moses: "Tell all the craftsmen whom I have endowed with skill to make the vestments for the consecration of Aaron as my priest . . .. using gold; violet, purple, and scarlet yarn; and fine linen." And the biblical description of the priestly garment contains the smallest of details. Including "two chains of pure gold formed into ropes", "a breast piece . . . made in gold, with violet, purple and scarlet . . . set in it four rows of precious stones: the first row sardin, chrysolite and green felspar; the second row, purple garnet, lapis lazuli and jade; the third row, turquoise, agate and jasper; the fourth row, topaz, cornelian and green jasper, all set in gold rosettes."

And so it is that today, fifteen years after Elvis Presley's death, his impersonators dress in his style, announce their stage entries with the same dramatic and evocative music; and the people who watch can be moved to that same fever pitch of excitement they might have reached had they been attending a concert given by the King of Rock and Roll himself. Yet it is not the charisma of the impersonator, the "Elvis for the night" which conveys the illusion, but the clothes, the props and all the accompanying pomp. And here the parallels with the worship of other faiths runs deep. Out of his vestments the priest is an ordinary mortal. In them he represents his God on earth. The vestments are frequently highly decorated with patterns and motifs symbolizing sacred ideas and the overall colour is dictated by the time of year or the occasion at which they are being used. A key vestment item worn within the Christian tradition is the stole, or scarf. Similarly with the followers of Elvis, the scarf is crucial. It is used as a stage prop and, as with Elvis in life, scarves touched or worn by the performer are sometimes handed out to members of the audience.

A priest is a go-between, a person who can channel something of an eternal unseen mystery through his person to the people. He is an initiate who must be called and must then study. Of the modern Elvis priesthood some talk of their conversions and callings and all spend a great deal of time studying and imitating the style and mannerisms of Elvis. Some are like the first apostles and feel they have an authority handed on to them by Elvis himself. They saw him in person and one, Douglas Roy, from Niagara Falls in Canada, was once invited on stage by Elvis himself and invited to sing *Hound Dog*. He was given a rabbit's foot by the King as a souvenir. Or was it not so much a memento as a symbol of authority or validation, similar to the Bible given to the priest at ordination or the episcopal ring and staff presented to a bishop at his consecration?

In some religions priests allow themselves to be taken over by a spirit from the other world. They dress in what they deem an appropriate manner and then change their whole personality and even their voice to be the channel whereby a spirit visits this world. An Elvis tribute is not a voodoo show. Elvis himself does not come from beyond the grave and possess the impersonator. Yet some impersonators do talk of a sense of singing in the spirit of Elvis and being "taken over". And fans hope they will be enabled to suspend their normal sense of disbelief and convince themselves that they have been in the presence of the King. Of late there have even been cases reported of claims that certain young Elvis impersonators are reincarnations of the Master. Elvis himself was fascinated by the possibilities of reincarnation. Why, certain mothers have asked, is it not possible for him to have returned in a new guise? The suggestion being that Elvis has returned through their own sons. But even if Elvis had chosen, or could choose, to return in this way, only one mother can have the true Elvis as a son. And which mother? Scope for dispute is endless.

Mike had been a regular soldier in the British army. He had seen action and experienced the full range of shock and grief which even the professional self-control of the modern fighter is unable to protect against when colleagues are killed close by. On entering civilian life he could not have sought a more different life. He decided to become an entertainer, specializing in giving, as he puts it, tributes to Elvis Presley. He purchased backing tracks which closely resemble the sound of the original Presley records and began to rehearse. He developed the gestures of the mature Elvis and, although his facial features are less rounded than the original, in his elaborate stage costumes, which are all reproductions in the style of Elvis originals, he succeeds in portraying much of his hero. The voice is harsher and less delicate, but there is no doubting the passion and emotion Mike pours into every song.

Mike has been an Elvis fan since he was a boy and feels he can relate to almost every one of Elvis's songs. He talks of how the message and comfort of Elvis, which comes through the music, sustained him through the traumas he experienced as a soldier. Stories have been told of men who have seen active service and felt the protective hand of God at work so positively in their lives that they have decided to dedicate themselves to God when the fighting is over, and have become priests. In a way it is something like that with Mike. His life is now dedicated to spreading the good news of Elvis and glorifying his memory and music.

Mike is wary about talking about his experiences in the army, but admits to having been caught up in a very public and bloody incident.

I had a sad loss in a certain situation and Elvis's music helped me through a great deal. I could not have managed without him, I really couldn't. I can't go into describing it any more but it was such a big shock. By listening to Elvis and going through the experience of grief and recovery with him, he brought me a relief and an outlet which I had never experienced before. I was still in the army and used to carry a little Walkman with me when I was having my rest periods. There were long hours of depression which other people just can't relate to and Elvis's music took the pressure away. It may sound a little stupid to other people, but even when I am performing now, there is some form of energy I can feel, I tend to get that extra push.

I am not an Elvis impersonator, that is a horrible idea to put across. My act consists of me giving my own personal tribute to Elvis, to keep his music and everything that was about Elvis alive. On average I practise between two and a half and three hours a day. My suits are made for me by my wife's aunt and I sew on all the sequins and rhinestones to my own designs.

We do not copy every design he had but we like to have a full range of suits to give variety. When I return to a pub or club, I don't want to go back dressed the same as before. As with his music he had such a vaste range of clothes, and I try to put this across.

I have moulded my hair to his style and dyed it black. It was dark brown, so that change didn't really matter. I have always had sideburns, even before joining the army, so there is nothing different there in my appearance.

Like a priest in the Christian church solemnly preparing himself to celebrate the eucharist, the devoted Elvis impersonator must also be in the right frame of mind to represent Elvis to the people. Without pushing the parallels too far or in an inappropriate manner, it is interesting to record how members of the Elvis "priesthood" talk about their preparation for their role. Many priests will not break the fast of the day until they have celebrated mass. Mike, for instance, will not touch alcohol before performing, and talks of his nervousness and the importance of getting everything right.

> When I am dressed as Elvis and about to perform, without a doubt I have a reverence for his memory. I have the same respect even when I am talking about him. Without this reverence or respect, there would be no way one could put on the act. I have watched the videos of his performances and seen what he went through. If you do not have a total commitment, you shouldn't be doing it.

In some traditions, the Roman Catholic being the main example, the church has said priests should not marry as the priestly vocation cannot, within one individual's life, coexist with any other. The Anglican church has found that where a wife supports her husband's vocation to the priesthood, together they form a strong partnership. There are, however, occasions when wives have not welcomed or accepted a husband's calling, and serious tensions have arisen. Mike's wife Denise was willing for her husband to follow the path he had chosen, but was unprepared, initially, for the consequences. "It took him over completely. He would do his performance and then afterwards continue in the part and forget he was married and had a wife sitting in the corner as he spoke to people. I thought Elvis was overtaking him. We went through a really bad patch when he started. Various times I told him to pack his bags and go." Mike acknowledges the dangers as he looks back: "It was getting dangerous, though I didn't realize it at the time. We were having arguments. Denise was being left out." Eventually after one very serious row, Mike saw how he was being so caught up in the role and so taken in by the adoration of his audiences, that he was in danger of losing his wife and family. Between them they decided on a solution. Denise would give her wholehearted support to Mike's new career as an entertainer, while he would agree that once off the stage, the performance stopped. "When I have performed, it finishes up there. I sit down and we are a family again. In fact Denise is now getting involved in the performances and has started to do some backing singing. She is good and I have more confidence when she is behind me. She still gets cheesed off with all the practice I do and the way I get nervous before a performance. But things are better." It is as hard for Mike now to contemplate a world without Elvis as it would be for a priest to contemplate a universe without a creator. "Basically all my life has been Elvis. Wherever I have been, all over the world, good times or bad times, Elvis has been there. The day he died, it felt like a part of me had gone. I cried my eyes out like thousands of others. It was so cruel. There was such an emptiness." But Elvis now lives on, on record, film, in the memories of his thousands of followers and in the actions of men like Mike. In the clothes, the vestments of Elvis, they re-create the living body, in flesh and blood, in remembrance of their hero.

The Elvis priesthood, if that is what it is, is not a simple priesthood of all believers in which any fan of Elvis has the right to represent him. First of all, it is a male priesthood. In the way that many church traditionalists argue that it is impossible for a woman to represent Christ at the altar, so it is said, it is absurd for a woman to stand in front of an audience and pretend to be Elvis. Was not his masculinity such an important ingredient of his style? Nevertheless there is at least one female Elvis, Janice Kucera. With her long blond hair she does not look the part, but the sound she produces has a believable Elvis timbre. She says she discovered her Elvis voice when she was walking, day dreaming of Memphis in the rain. "Magically out of the centre of me (maybe my heart and soul) this line rolled out loud: 'Ah, any place is paradise when I'm

with you. Baby I'd live deep in the jungle, sleep in the tree.'
Man, it was so Elvisie, and what a thrill." She saw Elvis
perform thirty-nine times and now, even after his death, talks
of being close to Elvis.

His spirit guides me. My audiences come to see Elvis and
when I am singing it's the King's voice they hear. Elvis is
my life, the very core of me and my sole inspiration. I truly
believe the Lord gave Elvis to the world as a gift, a gift to
the entertainment world of the greatest magnitude and the
likes of which we'll probably never see again.

A recent American guide to Elvis impersonators lists sixty-four
leading acts. It is just the tip of the iceberg, for, in addition
to the best-known semi-professionals, there are hundreds of
amateurs. Significantly, the guide, published by Pocket Books,
is entitled *I Am Elvis*. The entertainers profiled are not shy
about using the word "impersonator". They describe their
"calling" in many ways, but repeatedly express a deep
commitment and seriousness of purpose. Mike Moat, a thirty-
year-old Elvis impersonator based in New Jersey, says, "I take
what I do very seriously. This isn't done for kicks." Rick
Ardisano from Illinois believes, "impersonators should feel very
honoured that they can do Elvis." Sammy Stone Atchison sees
Elvis as the last great American hero, "all giving, all sacrificing,
all powerful in his endeavours. Elvis was the most charismatic
person ever on earth except for Jesus."

It is Clayton Benke-Smith who unashamedly borrowed the
words of St John's gospel to express his feelings. "In the
beginning there was the word, and the word was Elvis." He
talks of his dedication to his calling. "Any Elvis performer who
is dedicated to re-creating Elvis's mystique has to eat, sleep,
feel and act like the King."

Bruce Borders is the elected mayor of Jasonville in Indiana
as well as being an Elvis performer. He says he would like to
be remembered as a "man who loved God with all his heart,
and who helped others know that God loves them and cares

for them." Robert Bradshaw, from Illinois, while cautious of overstating the claims made for Elvis, adds, "he was an impressive person sent by God with a mission to lead and minister."

Louie Michael Bunch Junior is one of the younger impersonators and was only nineteen when he featured at the June 1990 Elvis Presley International Impersonators Association Convention in Chicago. He prepares for each performance by watching videos of Elvis concerts, trying to enter into the spirit of his idol. "Before I go on stage I usually say a prayer and thank the good Lord for giving me the talent and the opportunity to sing."

Dennis Wise braved the plastic surgeon's knife to perfect his stage illusion of Elvis. With his new looks and specially made replica suits, he is one of the busiest acts of the impersonator's circuit. He talks of his love for Elvis and how he has dedicated his life to him. "I am not here to take the place of Elvis, this could never be. I am here to bring back memories. I will perform wherever there are Elvis fans for as long as the good Lord gives me strength."

The Australian Ken Welsh, who appears on stage as Elvis under the name Elvin Eagle, believes that if Elvis had lived he would have brought peace to the world. "I believe there is a rock and roll heaven, and if there is, I'm sure Elvis is smiling, because wherever I'm performing in memory of the King, there are a lot of people honouring his memory."

Whether it is conscious or unconscious, the words used by the Elvis priests to describe themselves, their acts or their beliefs, frequently have a convincing religious ring. The words chosen by the Florida based impersonator Hans Vige to describe what he hopes Elvis would say about his act, are full of the resonances of the Christian eucharistic prayer of concecration. "This is my style, this is my music, this is part of my legacy, this is my gift to the world. Please continue to share it with me."

Bert Hathaway is a pharmacist by profession but an Elvis impersonator by calling. He vowed on the day Elvis died to do everything he could to keep the memory of his hero alive for ever. When he prepares himself for a show he says, "I can actually feel Elvis's presence with me and I become Elvis." He says of Elvis that he was, by far, the greatest person that has ever walked the face of the earth.

Ron Dye from Illinois expresses a similar devotion to Elvis and not just through his act. His home, like those of many fans, is full of memorabilia and he admits: "I live and breathe Elvis. I do it because I love the man. Elvis completely changed the course of musical history. He was sent by God for a purpose, to help during troubled times."

Ron "Elvis" Dye from Cresthill, Illinois, has a calling. Not to sing or appear on stage as Elvis, but to bear witness to his memory by dressing as Elvis did and living as he did. He sees himself as a messenger from Elvis, someone to "put the record straight when others put Elvis down."

One of Britain's most accomplished impersonators is Johnny Dumper who, unusually, is able to present tributes to Elvis at all stages of his career. Often impersonators, if they are older, concentrate on the latter years, or if younger, prefer the macho, rebellious look. He has also succeeded in persuading Elvis's old backing group the Jordanaires to sing with him.

There is no reliable estimate as to how many Elvis impersonators there are. One guess, often reported, is that there could be up to five thousand worldwide. This is probably an exaggeration if an Elvis impersonator is defined as someone who is more than a person who occasionally dresses in the style of Elvis, but actually makes money as an entertainer. There are many thousands of fans who copy his hairstyle and sideboards, but make no further attempt to represent Elvis and his talent and who certainly never get paid for their efforts.

One of the largest regular gatherings of impersonators and look-alikes is held to coincide with the Graceland August pilgrimage. The priestly caste congregates at a Memphis diner called Bad Bob's Vapors, for a competition. The rather noisy and scruffy diner, which claims the largest dance floor in Memphis, holds regular "talent" competitions, and most weeks of the year encourages country singers of varying degrees of talent to perform for its steak-chomping clientele. Come Elvis week in August, the place is bursting with Elvis replicas.

Comparisons between the vocation to the Christian priesthood and the urge to become an Elvis impersonator should not be pushed too far. Elvis impersonators do not have a pastoral role, nor, usually, do they have a teaching role. Neither do impersonators perform baptisms, marriages, or funerals. But who can tell what might happen in the future if the Elvis cult survives?

☆

EIGHT

Who Did He Say
That He Was?

Picture the scene, Elvis's opulent bathroom at Graceland. The King of Rock and Roll leans over the marble basin with a towel around his shoulders as a tall, dark talkative man tends to the star's famous hair. The man is Larry Geller, who was hired as Elvis's personal hairstylist in 1964 and stayed with him in that capacity, for three years. He was also the man brought in to fix Elvis's hair for his final appearance before his fans, as he lay in state at Graceland after his death.

Larry, however, was no ordinary hairdresser. He was Elvis's guide, his inspiration, his swami. Indeed he was frozen out of the Elvis camp by the Colonel and other members of the Memphis Mafia when they saw what a hold the hairdresser had over his client. He had the control and the influence of a guru. For years Elvis had had questions forming and exploding in his mind. He could not understand how a poor lad from Tupelo had become an international idol. Why him? What did he have that others did not? Was there some special purpose to his life that he had not yet grasped? Larry Geller introduced Elvis to answers.

Up until meeting Larry, Elvis's knowledge of religious matters was based on his childhood experience. He had been brought up in a gospel church. The message preached from the pulpit was a rigorous fundamentalism. Sin was real, as was divine punishment, God was to be feared, hard work was never to be shirked and God had blessed America. If there were not too many of those blessings in evidence in Elvis's bit of America, there was the covering message that the poor and the righteous could expect reward in the next life. If that was the message of the preachers, it was one to be learned, but the preachers themselves did not impress the Presley family. Elvis grew up with a certain scepticism when it came to church organisations and structures. Even ministers were suspect. On this earth the joy to be had in religion was not from the message, but from the music, the swaying gospel sound. Sometimes Elvis was taken to a travelling tent mission where the music and the beat, together with a riproaring message, brought a rare excitement to the drab lives of many families ground down by the years of economic depression.

So Elvis first heard music and felt its power and inspiration through the Christian faith of poor-town Tupelo. It was a faith to be experienced and felt and not one which demanded brain power. When Elvis suddenly found himself catapulted out of the secure life he knew, and then when his life was shattered by the death of his mother, he was confused. At which point, enter Larry Geller. His spiritual upbringing had been far more exotic. Although Jewish, his father was a member of an obscure sect, The Church of World Messianity, and a healer who used a Japanese system called Johrei. He was, says his son, one of the first New Agers. With this background, Larry, at the age of twenty-one, began his own spiritual quest. It followed an experience of rebirth in the desert near the Grand Canyon, a reawakening which he later compared to being struck by a bolt of lightning. He read the Bible, the works of eastern mystics, writers who looked at the "ancient wisdoms" and explored the occult. He studied theosophy, Taoism, the Cabala and the Judaism of his ancestors. By the time he met Elvis his mind was spinning with ideas which he wanted to share with the world. What better opportunity could he have than the chance to be in intimate contact with and feed ideas to a superstar who the world wanted to listen to?

Many of the ideas which were fed to Elvis and which he

enthusiastically devoured can be traced back to the curious nineteenth century religious teacher Madame Helena Blavatsky. Although largely dismissed as a fraud, she still has her followers within the Theosophical Society which she founded in 1875. Elvis was fascinated by her and claimed from the black and white photographs he saw of her that she resembled his mother. Her teachings included the idea of the existence of a secret doctrine or body of esoteric teaching which had been handed down through the ages by a brotherhood of adepts or mahatmas scattered throughout the world. The ancient wisdom of this master race had been fragmented and any profundities in surviving faiths and philosophies were lost pieces of the whole mystery. She believed in the study of all faiths and philosophies and the investigation of the spiritual or mystical powers latent in human beings. Her book, *The Secret Doctrine*, was recommended to Elvis, along with over twenty other esoteric works, by Larry Geller, who had quickly captured his client's imagination with talk of the deeper meaning to life. Amongst the other works Elvis read at his suggestion were books with such evocative titles as, *The Impersonal Life*, *The Tibetan Book of the Dead*, *The Mystical Christ*, *Through the Eyes of the Masters*, *The Life and Teaching of the Masters of the Far East*, *The Inner Life* and *Cheiro's Book of Numbers*. Elvis studied them eagerly, writing his own notes and questions in the margins. Once Elvis had grasped the idea that the Jesus of his childhood could have been just one of the great masters of history, it did not take him long to start wondering if he too was one of the chosen. Did not his extraordinary rise to fame and stardom hint that something about him was special?

Of all the works, the one he felt most attached to was *The Impersonal Life*. He handed out copies to friends like evangelical tracts. The book, it is claimed, although attributed to an early twentieth-century writer called Joseph Benner, contains a direct revelation from God.

Elvis also studied the teachings of the Indian Yogi Paramanhansa Yogananda, who came to the west in 1920 and died in the United States in 1952. Yogananda had learned the ancient secrets of Kriya Yoga described as "an instrument through which human evolution can be quickened." Yogananda said that he had come to reveal the complete harmony and basic oneness of original Christianity as taught by Jesus Christ and original Yoga. Elvis was introduced by Larry Geller to one of Yogananda's pupils who agreed to share the principles of Kriya Yoga with him. Elvis, however, did not have the patience to complete the course. He was too used to expecting instant results. He could not buy himself instant enlightenment, but he knew enough about meditation to know what its value might be. As to the practice of meditation, his attempts were probably sincere, but superficial.

Of his album *How Great Thou Art*, a collection of gospel hymns, Elvis said, "Millions of people around the world are going to hear this album. It's going to touch people in ways we can't imagine. And I know this album is ordained by God himself. This is God's message and I'm his channel. Only I can't be a channel if my ego is there. I have to empty myself so that the channel is totally pure . . . I'm not going to move out of this chair until I'm guided by that still, small voice within." Before recording the album, he meditated for half an hour to prepare. The result was a sound which, while proving both durable and popular with Elvis fans has also been dismissed contemptuously as "religious easy listening".

The story is told of Elvis having one profound religious experience, that of a vision of Christ and the Antichrist in the clouds over the Arizona desert. Larry Geller was with him at the time.

Tears streamed down his face and he cried out, "It's God, it's God! It's love. God is real. It's all true. I love God so much. I'm filled with Divine Love. It's beyond words and beyond the ego. I'll never doubt it again, God loves me. God is love itself.

"I saw the face of Stalin and I thought to myself, Why Stalin? Is it a projection of something that's inside of me?

Is God trying to show me what he thinks of me? Then your words about getting rid of the ego and all that played in my head, and I cried out to God, 'If that's really me, Lord, I want to die. All I truly want is you. Please, God, fill me with Yourself. Destroy me if that's what it takes.'

"And then it happened! The face of Stalin turned right into the face of Jesus, and he smiled at me, and every fibre of my being felt it. For the first time in my life, God and Christ are a living reality. Oh, God, Oh God."

And then, according to Larry Geller, Elvis paused and began to wonder what his fans would think if they could see him at that moment. Then his other travelling companions caught up with him and began to ask what was going on. "How do you explain to a non-believer when you just had a vision?" Elvis asked. "A vision when Almighty God touches you and reveals Himself? I saw the Christ and the Antichrist! Oh Lord."

In his latter years, Elvis had many questions in his mind about death and "the other side". His grief at his mother's funeral was intense and sometimes uncontrollable. And his mourning was witnessed by a media circus. At Gladys's funeral he threw himself on her coffin, hugging it and kissing it, speaking to it in the pet baby talk language he had used when talking with his mother in life.

That Elvis came to believe in reincarnation is suggested in a book about Elvis and his mother by Elaine Dundy. The book is called *Elvis and Gladys*.

Five months before Elvis's death, while he was waiting in his car outside Graceland for the gates to open, his eyes fell upon a woman standing in the crowd. He invited her into his house and the following letter, stamped with an affidavit, on display at the Elvis Presley Museum in Memphis, tells us the rest of the story:

"I met Elvis in early March 1977. In his own words I was a reincarnation of his mother (Gladys Love Presley). Love was also his name for me. In April 1977 he gave me this ring. It was a gift to his mother from him in 1955.

"These were Elvis Presley's own words. I never doubted him one moment. It is one of the first gifts for her.

"Sincerely,

"Ellen Marie Foster."

Also on display is the ring referred to in the letter. It is of eighteen-carat white gold with a small square-cut diamond surrounded by diamond chips resting in a delicate filigree setting.

We don't know what the proud nineteen-year-old gave his delighted mother as a birthday gift that April in 1955 twenty-two years before. If it was the same ring – and from its design nothing seems more appropriate – he had treasured it all this while. In giving it to her "reincarnation", perhaps he recaptured for a fleeting moment the pleasure he had felt in giving it the first time.

Elvis was much concerned too to find an explanation as to why he had lived and his brother Jesse had died. When she was alive their mother talked about Jesse as a person, a member of the family, even though he had not lived one day. Elvis came to believe that Jesse had been born to escort him to earth and that this was evidence of God's purpose behind his own life.

To take an interest in such ideas as reincarnation and meditation is unexceptional. Elvis however went further in his exploration of spiritual ideas, to the point where this question should be posed. Did he believe, as many of his fans appear to believe today, that he was a figure of comparable importance to Jesus?

Despite his upbringing in a fundamentalist Christian tradition, where doctrinal deviation was neither approved of nor encouraged, he had developed his own image of Jesus. Elvis, says Larry Geller, did not accept that Jesus was the only begotten son of God. He preferred to think that everyone had something of Christ in them and had the same potential. "Elvis felt that while on earth Christ revealed very deep, profound secrets, but that what we read today of what Jesus supposedly said is a watered-down version," wrote Larry Geller in his book, *If I Can Dream*:

> He thought that Jesus experienced everything that all people experienced, that he was the flower of humanity, that he suffered, and yet his suffering was ecstasy. Later in his life, whenever he felt that he was truly suffering, Elvis would say, "This is the way Jesus was. Did you ever see Jesus mentioned in the Bible laughing? Never. Not once does it say that Jesus smiled or laughed. That's because he had this compassion for other people. He knew where other people were at. He knew the sufferings of humanity. I understand that, and that's why I am who I am. That's why God put me on earth. That's part of my mission. Only today things are different. Today everything is technical."

Yet, according to Larry Geller, Elvis's ideas evolved further. Much influenced by Vera Stanley Adler's book, *The Initiation of the World*, he became fascinated with the idea of a group of spiritual masters called the "White Brotherhood", whose job it is to oversee human affairs.

> Elvis believed that he was working under the aegis of these masters, including Jesus. He felt somehow connected to them and thought that they had helped him, but not through messages or what some people today call channeling, because he wasn't into that. In Elvis's mind, his life was being directed divinely by the brotherhood of masters and illuminated beings, enlightened entities that have existed since time immemorial. And he truly felt that he was chosen to be here now as a modern day saviour, a Christ.
>
> Now, many people have misconstrued this to mean that Elvis thought he was Jesus, which is simply not true. It's important to remember that Christ is not Jesus's second name, Christ is a word that means truth, from *christos*,

Greek for "annointed one". Technically speaking, it's Jesus the Christ, not Jesus Christ.

Elvis's ideas shocked the upright church members of Memphis and his father found them hard to grasp; yet perhaps they were not too great a divergence from the religion of his youth. For although it was nominally Protestant, Christian and fundamentalist, Gladys herself held to many of the old superstitions about life which the church frowned upon, but which in practice it knew it could never eradicate and so attempted to absorb.

Elvis came to believe that the voice of his own conscience was the voice of God within him. At one stage he spent hours talking about his ideas and preaching to anybody who would listen. In the way that a Christian might wear a cross, Elvis also displayed his new spiritual interests in the form of jewellery. On his birthday in 1967, Elvis was given a Tree of Life medallion which he wore until his death, alongside his Jewish Star of David and Christian Cross of Jesus.

Elvis's image of himself as one of history's extraordinary people was reinforced by many of the people he chose to have around him. Larry Geller talked of his aura and the photographer Sean Shaver talks of sensing the "electric energy" flowing during his stage performances. Elvis spoke about the "Light of God" and writing of Elvis, Gail Brewer-Giorgio adopts a lyrical, mystical style.

Elvis believed that our "Light" (soul) came from the light of God, but that that Light (once spiritual) was now confined in the physical body – that same spiritual Light representing the sum total of all knowledge. Realizing this and practising this may explain why Elvis seemed to "Glow", and why so many millions were and are attracted to this special man, how they automatically love him. Elvis's Jesus connection obviously embraced the biblical "I am the way, the truth and the life: no man cometh unto the Father, but by me."

Because music is the international language – a language

that often bypasses the physical senses – Elvis was able to reach the world.

In terms of sheer numbers reached, the Elvis message, thanks to records, television and radio, has reached as many millions as has the Christian message, and in a much shorter time.

*

There were two men called Parker who had a controlling influence over Elvis: the one, the Colonel, Tom Parker, and the other a karate expert and devout Mormon, Ed Parker, who spent seventeen years as a friend, karate coach and confidant to the King of Rock and Roll. While the Colonel would have nothing to do with Elvis's personal exploration of spiritual ideas, thinking they distracted his boy from his real purpose, i.e. making money for the Colonel, Ed Parker, along with Larry Geller, was one of the people Elvis went to to test his ideas.

Ed Parker died thirteen years after Elvis, but in his writings he confirmed Elvis's fascination with all facets of the debate about the meaning of life and the universe. Once Ed told Elvis how he had seen an Unidentified Flying Object. He was in his native Hawaii at the time and recalled seeing a curious object travelling the night sky. Far from disbelieving his friend, Elvis capped the story. He too had seen a UFO. He had been with his father and had seen a circular object glowing in the evening sky above Graceland. It was, he said, a very intimate and sacred moment, and it had reminded his father of the curious incident of the blue light in Tupelo at the time of his birth.

"Could that light have been for me?" he asked Ed.

"Yes, most definitely," Ed replied. Later Ed was to write that with all the influence he had had on people, Elvis was involved in missionary work without realizing it and he must have been a special person to have come into the world in the way his father described.

Elvis also spent many hours listening to the tales of one man who claimed not only to have seen a UFO, but been aboard one. Elvis listened fascinated as he told him of his meetings with an alien from Planet Wolfe 359 in the Tythanian Galaxy, who could travel at 7.5 times the speed of light and who invited him aboard his spacecraft, *Rainbow X*.

As a Mormon, Ed Parker was particularly interested to learn that Elvis had a claim to a Cherokee Indian element in his ancestry. Ed talked of the American Indians being a remnant of the House of Israel. He said that the Indians talked of a time, which corresponded with the date of Christ's crucifixion, when The Great White Brother had come to America. He had taught people to live in love and peace and that he would return one day. He would return, so Ed suggested, when certain prophecies had been fulfilled. He convinced Elvis that they were living in the end time, and that the Great White Brother, the Christ, was due to return before very long.

Ed tells in his book, *Inside Elvis*, of a conversation they had had on the subject of reincarnation.

Elvis talked about the lost city of Atlantis, and he recounted to me some of the tales woven for him by people who were deeply involved in that train of thought. They had tried to convince him that he had been a great general in the city of Atlantis in a previous life. He asked me what I thought. I spoke bluntly. I told him that the concept of reincarnation was only viable if, in discussing reincarnation, you were talking about resurrection. And I asked him this question, "Christ was sent here on this earth to be the perfect example, is that correct?" His answer was yes. I asked, "Was Christ reincarnated or was he resurrected?" He replied, "Ed, I've never thought of it that way before." I said, "It's obvious, isn't it?" He asked, "What about these people who claim to have memories from a previous life?" "Well, Elvis, this is only speculation, but we might, as spirits, have been privileged to observe things that were transpiring here on the earth. If so, perhaps that's what they're remembering if, in fact, it's not a figment of their imaginations. But of this I am certain, if Christ, the perfect example, was not reincarnated, then you and I, my friend, only have to go through the test of life once."

In brief, Elvis's theology was a hotch-potch of pseudo-New Age esoteric ideas, layered upon a foundation of deep American South God-fearing Christian fundamentalism, mixed in with a pot-pourri of assorted superstitions picked up at his adoring mother's knees. It fermented in a bright, but untutored and undisciplined mind, into a confused set of notions. These notions suggested that Elvis himself was someone special, possibly a messianic figure. It was not such an improbable idea, Elvis felt, given the extraordinary and improbable things that had already happened to him, coming, as he did, from nowhere to win fame, glory and worldwide adulation. These ideas took root as some of those around him encouraged him on his "spiritual quest".

Before being introduced to the quasi-New Age ideas which were to come his way later in life, the young Elvis had a basic home-spun Southern gospel faith. It contained an element that suggested that if you were a good God-fearing American and prayed hard enough, God could intervene in your life and make the American dream come true. Interviewed in a teenage magazine in 1957 he had no doubts that if "you just have faith in God you will make it." No doubt he considered his own experience proof of that. "When I was 18," Elvis said, "I saw my Dad sitting on the edge of the bed with his head in his hands. Things were going so bad he couldn't see his way out. I prayed for a miracle and my prayer was answered." He went on:

I don't usually talk about these things because people might say I'm just using religion to impress them. Sure, I like to have a good time and do all the things other kids my age do. I'm no different from the rest. I like a movie, a swim, a drive up Main Street, a laugh, a stop at a drive-in for Cokes and shakes. I like to take a girl home on a cold night, stand on her porch, kiss her goodnight and try to keep from waking her folks up. That's why it kind of hurts me when they say I'm contributing to juvenile delinquency.

I'm no saint, but I've tried never to do anything that would hurt my family or offend God. If the rest of the "juveniles" in the country would try to use that formula, there wouldn't be any delinquency problem. I figure all any kid needs is hope and the feeling he or she belongs. If I could do or say anything that would give some kid that feeling, I would believe I had contributed something to the world.

Larry Geller, according to one member of the Memphis Mafia, was the man who put "all that weird shit into Elvis's head." Sam Phillips, however, the man who can be said to have discovered Elvis, and a serious man who, because of his background, one might suppose would be dismissive of any esoteric claims, is reported to have said of Elvis that he was an avatar of the Second Coming. An avatar is defined as one who descends to earth in incarnate form. A messenger of the Gods perhaps, or even a God taking human form? Alternatively a prophet or witness, a John the Baptist figure. Elvis would have known the word avatar. He would have been introduced to it when reading the work of Alice Bailey, one of the writers recommended to him by Larry Geller. Alice Bailey anticipates the coming of a special world teacher, an avatar, to shepherd in the New Age of enlightenment. It will be a time when fears of war, threats of famine and the dangers of pollution and planetary degradation will be removed. One definition of the New Age coined by a Christian writer goes as follows, "A smorgasbord of spiritual substitutes for Christianity, all heralding our unlimited potential to transform ourselves and the planet so that a New Age of peace, light and love will break forth."

It is curious to think of Elvis as a hippy New Ager. Indeed, the gun-carrying macho American boy would probably have had little time for the flower-power peace brigade. But he was fascinated by some of the underlying esoteric ideas, particularly those which he could seize upon in his attempt to understand his confused life. Why had he, of all people, been catapulted into stardom, a stardom which now had him trapped inside his luxurious Graceland prison? No wonder, after his death, fans began to speculate about the possibility that Elvis had faked his own death so as to return to being a normal member of the American public again. Elvis had no cultural empathy with the hippy New Agers, and was fiercely opposed to their use of illegal drugs, but he shared some of their root ideas. The idea that higher beings had come from Venus millions of years ago would not have seemed incredible to Elvis who had a firm belief in UFOs. Hadn't both he and his father seen one? He liked the idea of special masters appearing on earth with a mission. Did he not fit into that picture? Indeed did not his fans endow him with magical qualities? Had he not come from the humblest of beginnings to ascend a throne? His interests turned to telepathy, dematerialisation and reincarnation. If he was truly someone chosen, would he not find within him the powers to transcend the apparent laws of nature? He became fascinated with death and studied the timeless Buddhist tract, *The Tibetan Book of the Dead*. He took to arranging visits to mortuaries to talk to embalmers and others who prepare the dead for the final journey. He took to palmistry and found what he believed to be a highly significant cross on his hand, on the part known as the mound of Venus. Friends who telephoned him would be told how he had just had them in mind and was expecting a call. On Christmas Eve 1966 Elvis took Larry, who later recounted the story, together with Priscilla and another friend, upstairs at Graceland and began to talk about God. Priscilla was very sceptical about Elvis's spiritual interests. Elvis then suggested the four of them pray and spend some moments in meditation. Suddenly a light in the ceiling flashed on. "See," he said, turning to Priscilla, "This is what I've been trying to tell you about. How did that light go on?" Elvis was as convinced that the occurrence had not been a power line fluke as Priscilla was that it had been.

There is no evidence, however, that Elvis stuck to any demanding or rigorous esoteric or occult discipline for very long. He explored various traditions of meditation but wanted results too quickly. When it came to matters "out of this world" he still wanted to take care of business in a flash. Only at the martial arts, a physical pursuit with a spiritual dimension, did he make progress.

He did, however, make frequent use of numerology, and Cheiro's *Book of Numbers* was a much thumbed volume in his collection. To the uninitiated numerology appears neat, plausible and yet obviously bogus. How is it that by ascribing certain numbers to letters of the alphabet and working out from the letters of a person's name what his or her number is, that one can have any insight into their character? It seems even more unlikely than astrology. Are there not different alphabets, do not people have so many different names, formal names, pet names and so on, that coming to any coherent conclusion is impossible? Whatever an outsider's doubts, Elvis was convinced and played the numbers game frequently. Yet Albert Goldman, a sceptic in such matters, did point out in his book on Elvis that Elvis discovered that his number was eight. However, he was displeased with this for some reason and found another way of calculating his number. He arrived at both five and six, but was still not satisfied, wishing to be a ten, like his father.

Albert Goldman, who attracted both praise and savage criticism for his best-selling biography called simply, *Elvis*, dismisses Elvis's esoteric diet in a typical tirade.

Heavy! Right? The real hard-core mumbo jumbo.
    It never makes any difference when these books are written because they are always composed of the same banal or preposterous ideas in the same familiar code phrases . . . The reader is always being hailed, or better, haled, by pseudo-biblical prophet voices that cry out with the urgency of a great revelation. Then, as they maunder on for page after page of empty prose or kooky verse or abandon language in favour of diagrams, paradigms and arrangements of lotus blossoms, you realise that you've been had again

by the spiritual hucksters, the heavenly con men, the charlatans of the soul.

Another one of the books on Larry Geller's list which Elvis studied with considerable interest was *The Inner Life*, by Charles Leadbeater, a disciple of Madame Blavatsky. Written in the first decade of the twentieth century it talks of the Lords of the Flame, the Children of the Fire-mist, the great beings who came down from Venus nearly 18 million years ago to help and to lead the evolution of humanity. As time passed and mankind evolved, the Lords of the Flame, it is said, left Earth to found other civilisations in the universe, but, said Leadbeater, one remained who holds the position of "KING who guides and controls all evolution upon this planet". Under the King are the few highly advanced men of the Great White Brotherhood. Leadbeater also introduces the Lord Maitreya, who, he says, western people call the Christ since he took the body of Jesus for three years. Elvis would have found Ed Parker's ideas meshing with those of Leadbeater. One can picture an excited but confused Elvis lying back in his bed at Graceland and wondering where he fitted into the great scheme. Was he Great Master, one of the White Brotherhood, an advanced assistant?

When Larry Geller eventually left the inner circle, many of the books which Elvis had and which had been recommended to him by Larry, were taken and burned. The ideas, however, continued to smoulder in Elvis's mind for ten increasingly difficult and isolated final years. And towards the end of Elvis's life, Larry again played an important part as confidant to the troubled star. One notion in particular Elvis had had no problem in taking on board. Had he not from childhood had little time for ministers and formal religion? The idea which Elvis particularly cherished was that there was part of God, the God potential, in everyone. And perhaps some chosen people were a little more God like than others?

Of all the books in his collection there was one which Elvis turned to more than any other, even after many of his other books had been destroyed, *The Impersonal Life*. During the filming of *Spinout* in 1966, Elvis was full of the enthusiasm of a new religious convert. He talked esoteric ideas constantly, and every spare moment during the shooting of this, his twenty-second movie, he bombarded his co-star Deborah Walley with his ideas.

Larry Geller attributes the impact of the book on Elvis to the interpretation of God and his purpose which differed from any Elvis had yet encountered. The book expressed ideas which had been latent in Elvis but which he had never found the means to express. Mankind and the universe were described as reflections of the Creator's idea and all part of a single entity.

> The Key is
> To think is to Create, or
> As you think in Your Heart, so it is with you . . .
> You have within all possibilities.

In his book *If I can Dream*, Larry Geller wrote,

> To begin to understand his life, Elvis had to go beyond his childhood teachings. Among his relatives were people who believed that any book but the Bible was sinful, so it's easy to see how without some guidance Elvis might never have discovered the words that changed his life. *The Impersonal Life*, which stated that all knowledge served some purpose, that even people of flawed character have something to teach, opened the door for him, removing the restrictions imposed by organized religion. He saw that one didn't have to be a preacher or other religious authority to teach, and that the Bible wasn't the only book that recorded God's word or offered hope for man; in fact, it wasn't even the oldest.
>
> For someone like Elvis, who had wondered where he fitted into the scheme of things, what his purpose might be, what meaning lay behind the improbable and extraordinary events in his life, a passage such as this spoke very clearly: "When you have found The Kingdom, you will likewise find your

place in It, realizing . . . that your work was all laid out for you from the beginning, and that all that has gone before has been but a preparation and a fitting of your human personality for that work." In other words, knowledge promised an understanding that Elvis's life wasn't a fluke or an accident, and despite whatever doubts he felt about his deservedness, all of his life was in fact a preparation for the present and the future. Elvis suddenly came to believe that he had a purpose.

Elvis's first cousin Harold Loyd is a very down to earth individual who plays down the Elvis interest in the esoteric. He says,

Yes, Elvis did study astral projection and other different religions, but didn't get into them. He was raised in the Assembly of God church, and that's where he was raised up and he didn't vary from that. He studied other things, I'm sure. I am not sure I understand why he got to be so big and I really don't know why the fans keep coming back. He certainly had what it took as an entertainer. But he was also a humble man. He kept in touch with ordinary people.

But Harold probably never saw the side of Elvis which Larry Geller and others saw. Harold is a good, solid, unsophisticated man who would probably have no interest in exploring Larry Geller's reading list. So why would Elvis have ever shared his more unusual and eccentric thoughts with him? As a family member, Elvis would probably have been reluctant to share his Captain Marvel secret fantasies with someone who might have laughed at him. He only dared mention his inner thoughts when there were those in his entourage keen to encourage him.

When Elvis died it is said he was reading *The Face of Jesus*, a book about the shroud of Turin, which, at the time of his death had not been subjected to the scientific tests which were interpreted as proving it to be a medieval fake. Other sources, however, suggest that the last book Elvis saw on this earth was an astrological sex manual.

To a lot of fans, Elvis's meandering esoteric thoughts are of little interest. He speaks to them through his music. His legacy is the music and the image. That he had some wider messianic purpose is so much nonsense. And yet there are other fans who derive so much spiritual experience from their devotion to Elvis they feel impelled to look for an explanation as to why this might be. And where better to start looking than where Elvis himself began to look for explanations?

NINE

☆

Resurrection

This risen Elvis has been seen through the United States, in stores, petrol stations, even hitching lifts. He has been seen at Graceland and photographs have been published to prove it!

The explanations of these hundreds of reports of Elvis having cheated death fall into four categories. The most down to earth explanation is that honest witnesses have spotted or photographed some of the hundreds of people who look like Elvis. Many of his fans adopt his style of dress, have dyed their hair and wear sun glasses. Another explanation is that Elvis faked his death, and sometimes sneaks out of hiding to see the world. The third explanation is that Elvis is sighted as a ghost or a resurrected being. Like Jesus he has defeated death. The fourth explanation is that people who claim supernatural encounters with Elvis are deluding themselves or suffering from some psychological condition which leads to delusion.

Janice Kucera, the female Elvis impersonator, tells a strange story. Her infatuation with the star took her to Memphis when Elvis was alive and she has kept in touch with members of his family since. It was in 1983, a week before Christmas, that she was sitting at her kitchen table while her mother was cooking supper. She had just been speaking on the telephone to Elvis's Uncle Vester when she noticed a man looking in the south kitchen window. "It was Elvis's image! It was his forehead, cheekbones and nose on the window screen. The next day I went outside and all the limbs on the evergreen tree behind the window were scorched and singed." The image remained on the screen for four years.

Julian Campo never met or even saw Elvis Presley in person yet claims to have had several spiritual encounters with him since his hero died. Julian came to live in the United States from Sicily when a boy of twelve. His teenage years coincided with the years of Elvis's youthful, rebellious popularity. Julian heard Elvis perform on record and film and quickly identified with the sound and image. It was not until 1986, however, that Julian reports the spiritual encounters. On one occasion Julian had a vision of Elvis in a jumpsuit encouraging him to persevere with his performances as an Elvis impersonator, musician and actor. In another contact Elvis told Julian to start writing songs. In a third contact Julian was told to go to Graceland to pray by Elvis's grave. There, the message which came to Julian was the instruction to "be more humble to the Lord". He took the words to mean that he should continue with his act as an impersonator but be more humble in himself in each performance and in his contacts with people.

Kiki Apostolakos believes there have been many times in her life when Elvis has spoken to her and warned her of events. She tells a story of an event which she witnessed and experienced during one of the candlelight vigils at Graceland to mark the anniversary of Elvis's death. She was standing by a picture of Elvis on the small marble shrine on the steps of the pool, holding her candle. In her mind she was talking to Elvis about how much she missed him. It was a calm, still night, but the flame suddenly moved, flickered and went out, as if someone had touched it. She relit the candle from another and began to walk away. On meeting a friend she suddenly felt gripped by the conviction that Elvis had been trying to tell her something. "Something is going to happen in the house. Maybe it is Aunt Delta who is unwell." Her friend was disbelieving, "Are you crazy?"

"I hope things are all right," Kiki said, "but listen to me."

Then Kiki began to cry. Her mind began racing with

thoughts of Elvis. She felt such overwhelming despair that she did not want to continue living. She shared her thoughts and was reassured. "Kiki, we are here and must be thankful for what we have."

Then they heard the news. Aunt Delta was sick. The ambulance had been called for and she was taken to hospital where she was kept for three days.

One story, oft repeated by fans, which has now become an Elvis folk legend, is that when the space shuttle landed from one of its missions at Edwards Air Force Base, Elvis's kindly face appeared in the stars of the night sky and he was seen to stretch out a protective arm to guide the space-craft home.

"I wouldn't say I have seen Elvis since he died," says Marie, "but I feel his presence. Every time I go to an Elvis function I feel his presence, or when I am in the house alone playing his music. A lot of times if I have worries in life, I feel he helps me out. He has brought a lot of fans closer to God. Nine out of ten fans say their favourite Elvis music is the gospel music."

A story is told of a young girl in a coma in hospital. The doctors and her family feared she would not recover consciousness. She was on the edge of death. Then she was seen holding her hands out calling the name of "Elvis". She recovered and later talking to her parents asked, "Why didn't you leave me when Elvis was calling me? He was taking me up there." Interpreting such a story, fans do not claim it is Elvis who has the power to heal, but God empowers Elvis, they say, to come into people's lives, even their dreams.

Aaron, the dedicated Elvis fan from Southampton, has felt the comfort of Elvis at a time of stress. He was waiting anxiously outside a hospital ward for news of his son Kenny, who was about to undergo an important operation. Kenny is visually handicapped and the operation was to restore an element of sight. "It was the night before the operation, and I was about to go to sleep, when I felt somebody touch my shoulder. I knew straight away who it was because there was this lovely warm feeling and it was as though somebody was telling me, 'Don't worry, everything will be all right.' And he had the operation the next day and everything was all right, because he saw again."

Pam remembers Kenny's operation as being a time of great stress and recalls another incident which she took to be a sign of understanding and comfort from Elvis. For a break from waiting in the hospital for news, she and Aaron went for a walk around Exeter. They had never been to the city before, but found themselves walking from the hospital in the direction of a bookshop which they found "ablaze with Elvis books. I suppose in one way we had been spiritually guided there by Elvis. Knowing how much Kenny thinks of Elvis as well, that might have pushed us in there."

Pam tells the curious tale of the poster that fell from the wall of their flat one Easter Monday. Their home is full of Elvis pictures and souvenirs. They even have a life-size cardboard cut-out Elvis which they put on display when fellow Elvis fans come round for meetings. So one poster falling off the wall might not be said to be unusual. However, when Pam picked the poster up from the floor she saw the writing on it, "Easter Greetings from Elvis".

Pam says one such occurrence can easily be dismissed as coincidence, but remembers other strange occasions. They were sitting with friends talking about Elvis one August. The evening had turned into early morning and they were still chatting. "Then all of a sudden this picture just whizzed over from the shelf. It didn't drop, it flew about six feet across the room. We looked at each other and I went cold. We didn't say anything for three or four minutes. I couldn't understand it as there was no wind. Eventually one of us picked it up and in due course we all went our separate ways to bed."

Pam and Aaron also talk of the night Aaron saw one of their posters glowing. Not in a ghostly manner, but it was sufficiently unsettling for Aaron not to be able to sleep. And again they talk of a photograph which seems to fall as an omen. The first time it fell it heralded the news that a friend they had helped get to Graceland had died. On another occasion its fall coincided with the death of Elvis's favourite horse.

Harold Loyd recalls how when he was alive Elvis had a "sort of magnetism".

> I could be sitting in the room at Graceland, with my back to the door, and he would come in and I would sense his presence before hearing or seeing him. It was like ESP, sort of eerie.
>
> When I go in the house I can still feel that presence strongly. And also I can sit across the street and look across at the grounds and if I get to think hard I can almost see him up there riding one of the horses in the pasture. I saw that so many times when he was alive. But I have to concentrate.

Curious sightings did not start after Elvis's death. When he was still alive, Harold Loyd recalls meeting a woman who claimed to have been visited by Elvis's mother Gladys. The woman talked of how she visited Gladys's grave, placed flowers on it and communicated with her spirit, and how on one occasion Gladys appeared in person. As Harold Loyd remembers the end of the story, the woman became obsessed with the idea that she was being followed by a black panther and was taken away for hospital treatment. Harold recalls other stories of individuals with religious mania of some form arriving at Graceland with messages, they said, from God.

Some of the sightings of Elvis could simply be explained by turning to the experience of Ray Kajkowski who, while attending a fifties party in 1987, discovered a talent for impersonating the King of Rock and Roll. He shaved off his beard and began to develop the appearance. Friends and workmates who heard the rumours that Elvis had been seen in Kalamazoo, Ray's home town, became convinced that people were really seeing Ray in his new persona. On a visit to Graceland, Ray once attracted an astonished crowd of autograph hunters and when he walked into the pool room, a woman fainted at the shock of coming face to face with the man she thought was dead.

A similar experience has been reported by another Elvis look-alike, Russ Howe. One day he went fishing in upstate New York. The quiet afternoon away from it all turned into a media event when word spread that Elvis Presley had been spotted alive and well and fishing the same lake.

The following story, however, falls into the third category of explanation, Elvis, the man who faked his death. On the morning of the 1987 anniversary of the death of Elvis Presley's mother, two Elvis fans were walking in the cemetery in Memphis where Gladys had first been buried. They saw a man in a cap with his eyes shielded by dark glasses. As they passed by they both recognized him as Elvis.

As well as the thousands of portraits and action shots of Elvis which fans put on display, there is another style of picture which many cherish. They are the pictures of Elvis in some ethereal, imaginary, heavenly setting. Sometimes he is at prayer, other times glowing in a mystical light.

One fan said of a poster in her collection, "It reminds me of when Elvis died and went to heaven, he is standing by the gates of heaven looking down on his millions of fans all over the world. And the scenery in the poster reminds me of how heaven might look. As soon as you look at the picture you get the feeling of heaven."

In a black humoured vein, there are these lines from the song *Jesus Mentioned* by Warren Zevon:

> Can't you just imagine
> Digging up the King
> Begging him to sing
> About those heavenly mansions
> Jesus mentioned.

Yet a possibility is debated that would fill loyal Elvis fans with horror − that Elvis now rots in hell. Elvis, it is argued, for all his clean image and supposed good works, was an unrepentant sinner and hypocrite. No story of a deathbed recantation of his selfishness and excesses is ever told, and if it is the case that eternal damnation is reserved for those who sin and show no remorse, then that must surely be Elvis's destiny. And what of the words of Jesus that it is easier for a camel to pass through the eye of a needle than for a rich man to enter the kingdom of heaven? Was not Elvis fabulously wealthy? In his book *Dead Elvis*, Greil Marcus writes of going to a no-holds-barred debate held in the course of a seminar in 1982 in Memphis, attended by Christian Elvis fans. The question of Elvis's ultimate eternal destiny was argued over by people who were in no doubt that following judgement everyone was destined for one or other place, up or down, bliss or burning. Greil Marcus then writes the following:

Punk has fixed on the same question. In the fanzine *Flipside*, one comes across a Raymond Pettibone cartoon showing a decedent in white gown and angel's wings, tears streaming down his face: "You're just faking! Elvis is here; we know it. Tell us where he is! Show us Elvis!" A neosurrealist magazine arrives in the mail with a picture of Elvis in bat wings printed on the mailer. "All dressed up like an Elvis from Hell," runs a line from a Gun Club song: it's an image that calls up Jim Jones of the People's Temple, who so clearly modelled himself on the post-comeback, black-helmeted Presley. *Money Fall Out the Sky*, by Cool It Reba, a New York post-punk band, is about pop success; after covering the financial side of the issue, the singer gets down to cases:

> I want to live – like Elvis
> Drive a car – like Elvis
> I wanna sleep – like Elvis
> Walk around – like Elvis
> Take drugs – like Elvis
> Make love – like Elvis
> Go to hell – like Elvis.

It is on the dark side of the human psyche that there is to be found another pop star whose life has been accorded a spiritual significance after death. If Elvis is the bright star of the morning, signifying hope and promise, Jim Morrison is the star of the evil hour. His grave at Père-Lachaise in Paris, the most famous final resting place in France, attracts fewer people than Graceland's meditation gardens, but more vandals and a different kind of grafitti.

> "The older get older, as the young get stronger.
> May take a week, or may take longer.
> They got the guns,
> We got the numbers."
> "Free dope forever."
> "It's better to burn out than fade away!"
> "Anarchy"
> "Jim's not dead."

Jim Morrison devotees, although fewer in number than Elvis followers, can be equally dedicated. Some dress in his style. Most seem to emulate the lifestyle, including the alcohol and hard drugs. For like Elvis, Jim Morrison died of a heart attack, believed to have been brought on by a drug overdose; only in Jim Morrison's case the drugs were alcohol and heroin.

Jim Morrison died in 1971. He was called the Lizard King. The lizard and snake, he explained, are equated with the subconscious forces of evil. The snake embodies everything that we fear. He also proposed himself as his generation's sacrificial lamb. Morrison was an icon of the darker side of life.

However different the two men were in their proclaimed purpose, they have one final thing in common. Many years after their death, they are still being mourned deeply. In looking for explanations for the behaviour of Elvis fans, the author Dr Raymond Moody, examines the course that bereavement can sometimes take. The psychological literature, concerning grief and bereavement, he says, is rife with descriptions of phenomena which closely resemble the psychic experiences concerning Elvis Presley. Some known manifestations of grief and bereavement are: shock and numbing, denial, sadness, preoccupation with the image of the deceased, psychosomatic disturbances, establishing a "shrine" for the departed person, and "anniversary reactions". These manifestations can be seen to correspond with some of the activities of Elvis fans, particularly those concerning images and shrines. In his book, *Elvis After Life*, Dr Moody relates some of the "supernatural" appearances of Elvis to this thesis. He quotes the case of a police officer who finds his runaway son using information conveyed to him in a dream by Elvis Presley. Also the instance of the parents of a child who find they can accept her death more readily because the spirit of Elvis welcomed her into heaven. And, along with many others, he tells the story of a mother, terrified of being alone for the birth of her baby, who finds comfort and joy in the presence of Elvis;

> Regardless of whether any such experiences are finally "real" or not, they frequently occur in the context of mourning and bereavement. Accordingly it makes perfect sense to consider, when one is studying supposed psychic experiences, and to be sensitive not only to the apparent peculiarities of sensory perception and/or cognition with which they are associated, but also to the emotional context of human grief and bereavement in which they occur.

To many thousands of Elvis fans around the world, the death of Elvis was a shattering blow. Many talk of their feelings of loss as if a close member of the family had died. Dr Moody concludes, "One cannot come to an understanding of these experiences without taking into account the fact that they involve a charismatic celebrity who was truly on a first-name basis with the whole world. He left his own unique imprint on them as he did on everything he touched. And in doing so, he managed to cast his spell over all of us and for all time."

TEN

☆

The Church Militant

All religions have, in time, divided into churches and denominations. In the case of the Elvis cult the initial big divide is an essential one. It revolves around the fundamental question, is Elvis really dead?

There are those who say that, without a doubt he is, and it would have been a cruel, unforgivable trick for Elvis to have played if it is ever shown he is still alive; and there are those who say he is not, and that Elvis faked his own death for very good reasons; he may, one day when it is safe for him to do so, return to his public.

Both sets of fans are devoted to his music and the perpetuation of the legend which abruptly came to an end in August 1977, but they take a fundamentally different approach when it comes to describing and explaining that end.

A whole industry has grown up around the "Elvis is alive and well" theory. Sightings of Elvis have at some stages reached almost epidemic proportions. A telephone hotline was set up in the United States to both monitor claims of sightings and relay news to anxious fans. Stories have become increasingly absurd, especially in the tabloid press. An article published in the more serious British newspaper, *The Guardian*, in 1990, was a good summation of the scene. It was written by the paper's correspondent Martin Walker and by-lined Washington DC.

139

Meanwhile, at the fast food joints and gas stations on the Interstates of America, and places where witnesses are too hurried to linger and confront him, Elvis has been seen by hundreds.

Or so you hear when you call the Elvis hot-line.

Dial 900-246-ELVIS from any American phone and you can join "the central processing system to collect and broadcast Elvis sighting reports".

Elvis is big business. Last year's phone-in campaign recorded 1.5million callers, including sightings, best wishes to Elvis, and callers who just wanted to hear the latest reports.

On the 900 telephone exchange, each caller was charged $2 for the first minute and 95 cents for each minute after that. So 1.5 million calls was a minimum $3 million for Infotainment, the California-based company which specialises in entertainment by phone.

"This is a nationwide effort to determine if Elvis is really alive," says the tape when you dial the Elvis number. "You can record a personal fan message for Elvis or his spiritual soul."

Press button one on the phone and you hear "the mysterious no-label studio tape" of unreleased Elvis recordings.

Press button two and you can hear the latest sighting reports.

"I believe he's really alive," says Mary from Pittsburgh, and Tammy from Atlantic City wants to say that Elvis "had the greatest spiritual effect on people since Jesus Christ".

Press button three and record your own sighting. Press button four to buy a copy of the studio tape – which includes a glutinous version of *Are You Lonesome Tonight?*

"We are neutral on whether Elvis is alive. We have an open mind. There are photographs, reports of angels, impressive stuff," says Barry Paddock, director of Starbridge Communications, a subsidiary of the Infotainment Company . . . and he insists, "This is a serious and respectful operation."

Rarely an issue passes of the supermarket tabloid press without a claim that a "galactic Elvis fathered my baby" or "Elvis flew my UFO". There are books which claim Elvis faked his death and is now living a quiet life in Alaska, Hawaii or Key West. With Graceland now outdoing George Washington's home as a tourist attraction, Elvis dead is threatening to become bigger box office than Elvis alive.

One of the most elaborate cases yet devised to show that Elvis Presley is still alive is that compiled by Gail Brewer-Giorgio. To convince her readers she points to a whole range of "evidence" ranging from the alleged mis-spelling of Elvis's middle name on his tombstone to numerous photographs of Elvis which she believes were taken after his reported death. She also produces a tape of a voice, claimed to be that of Elvis, recorded after August 1977. Although she claims that Elvis is alive she does not in any way feel cheated by the hoax. Indeed her final words in her book, *The Elvis File*, are these:

> God bless you, Elvis. Whatever be the truth − whether Elvis is alive, whether all the "evidence" is but a series of giant coincidences − Elvis Presley was/is a giant star in the universe, a beloved son, father, husband, friend, American patriot − and a "Light" to whoever has paused to bask in its warmth. Elvis, you did indeed open up the window of your soul!
> This is not the end.

For a fan to claim that Elvis is still alive does not mean he or she dismisses the spiritual in Elvis's life. Indeed the comparisons between Elvis and Jesus are made with equal daring by both those who are sure he is dead and those who feel that he is living. Gail Brewer-Giorgio places much weight on the fact that Elvis read and owned a copy of the book *The Passover Plot*. This book, by Hugh Schonfield, was first published in 1965. It attempts to show that Jesus did not intend to die on the cross but to fake his own death. Gail Brewer-Giorgio implies that the book could have given Elvis the idea of faking his own withdrawal from public life. The spelling of the middle name Aaron on the gravestone is seen of enormous significance. It was Elvis's way of showing that he was/is still alive. There are even fans who say there are no bodies buried at Graceland at all as the graves are aligned north-south and not east-west as is customary. Once fans get deep into the mystery of Elvis's alleged death, they produce all kinds of problems and imponderables. What it all amounts to is that there is a significant group of followers of Elvis Presley who are convinced that he had to disappear for his own safety, some saying that his work as an undercover anti-drugs agent had put his life at risk. However, some fans argue, Elvis will return and 1993 is the suggested date. This will be sixteen years since he left the world and, it is pointed out, Jesus spent sixteen years on this earth which are now unaccounted for.

In *The Passover Plot*, the author says that Jesus truly believed he had a messianic mission. He was well versed in the Jewish scriptures and knew the prophecies of the books of the Old Testament. His carefully planned mission, starting with his baptism in the river Jordan, was intended to make all the prophecies come true. Even his apparent death on the cross was pre-arranged. And the story is not told to prove that Jesus was a fraud, any more than to say that Elvis in faking his death proves he had no special messianic purpose. Fans opposed to this line of thinking have long ago dismissed Gail Brewer-Giorgio's scenario as absurd; as for the tape she released of Elvis speaking after August 1977, the fans say they have shown it to be a fake by finding the true identity of the recorded voice.

If Elvis is still alive and well, where is he? Theories abound, and if his intention was to walk the streets of his native land incognito, he has certainly failed. When claims of sightings are made, fans are clear they have seen Elvis, dressed in the same clothes, even admitting to some his identity. There is the case of Sivle Nora, a mystery figure whose extraordinary name is an anagram of Elvis Aron. He is said to be the real Elvis in disguise. And then there is John Burrows, another supposed mystery figure who some claim to hold the key to Elvis's secret!

The hidden Elvis has supposedly made telephone calls from his self-imposed exile and even appeared on stage as an impersonator, impersonating himself. Fans split into the two camps over the question, who is the singer known as Orion? While one group was willing to accept that Orion was really an entertainer called Jimmy Ellis who sounded very much like Elvis, others were convinced that Orion was indeed Elvis himself, making his comeback after having gone into hiding. Orion released a record called *Down in Mississippi*. The last verse goes like this:

> Down in Mississippi, not far from Tupelo,
> Beneath the magnolia tree, and an old dusty road,
> Oh, I sing and play my guitar, and sit in the shade,
> And my blue suede shoes are home at last
> In this Mississippi clay.

The name Orion comes from the novel published in 1977 by Gail Brewer-Giorgio which tells the story of a rock and roll star who fakes his own death. Even though the real Jimmy Ellis has admitted to having sung as Orion, there are still fans who insist there are two Orions and Jimmy is just the front for one of them. The other is Elvis!

While there are no conclusive figures, it would appear that those fans who doubt the reports of Elvis's death are in a minority. How great a minority is unclear, but a Gallup Poll conducted in Canada in the eighties might give a guide. It was conducted amongst a general sample of the population and not merely among Elvis fans. Ten % of more than one thousand polled said they doubted Elvis died in 1977 and 5% said they believed he was still alive. In Britain a recent poll finding suggests 13% of the population consider Elvis might be living. If Elvis fans had been polled exclusively, the figures would probably have been higher, but not so significantly as to show the doubters to be in the majority. Further evidence to show that there are many fans who have not accepted the idea of Elvis being dead comes from the graffiti on the Graceland wall, and the testimony of many of the visitors. "I did not know him and I am too young to have seen him, yet I feel I know him"; as a result Kim from Los Angeles travelled half-way across the American continent to visit Graceland. "I wanted to see where he lived and the things that were important to him when he was here." Kim, however, has not accepted the idea that Elvis is dead. She has no commercial axe to grind and has never written a bestseller on the subject. She is one of the many fans who feels Elvis could still be alive today. Had he faked his death? In a sense, yes:

> He was with the CIA and got real involved with them and they relocated him. It was his only way of getting away from the public and living a different kind of life. He even said once that he had fulfilled all his dreams. Now he probably wanted to live like a normal person. And the CIA relocated him so that he could become a regular person and not be in the public eye all the time.
>
> If he has passed away he will always live in my heart and spirit. I even feel him now in spirit when I am watching a movie or listening to a record.
>
> He was religious, and so am I, and I touch base with him there. When I hear him sing about God I feel comfortable with him, I feel good. In some ways he brings me closer to God. He raises the spirits up.

The question as to whether Elvis is alive or dead causes deep division and distress. Kiki, one of the most dedicated Elvis fans, would be devastated if she ever learned that Elvis had deceived his fans. "He couldn't stay away from his fans so long. I know he is dead. To say he faked his death is a disgrace to his memory, to his daughter, to his family. They saw him in the coffin. They touched him. Elvis couldn't treat people like this."

Marie is in no doubt in her mind that Elvis died. She cannot believe that Elvis would put his fans through the great distress

of grief deliberately to fool them. Mike, the British entertainer
who pays tribute to Elvis through re-enacting Elvis's songs,
is outspoken on the idea that Elvis might still be alive, having
hoodwinked his loyal fans.

> If I heard that he had not died, but was hidden away
> somewhere away from the public I would be totally
> disillusioned. My belief in the whole man and his music
> would be destroyed. I would personally be gutted. I would
> finish completely what I am doing and disown him. To have
> deceived so many thousands of loyal people would be beyond
> contempt. Obviously there would be a lot of people happy
> that he was alive. But I think for him to have created the
> illusion of death would have really required a warped mind.

If the major doctrinal split in Elvisdom is between those who
believe he faked his death and those who believe he truly died,
there are many other subdivisions. Jennifer Walker's first
explanation as to why there are so many fan clubs is simple:
there are just too many fans to fit into two or three main
organisations. There are other discernible reasons, however,
and these parallel the way other churches have split into smaller
groups. Some divisions merely reflect geography: as well as
the USA, Canada, Great Britain and Australia have
organisations of fans. One American magazine claims it reaches
fans in fifty US states and seventy-three foreign countries. Yet
there are also subdivisions which have evolved for other
reasons. Sometimes there have been personality clashes and
clubs have divided. On other occasions fans have differed as
to exactly what they should be doing to honour the name of
Elvis. Should they spend more time raising money for charity,
or would they be best employed defending Elvis's reputation
against public attack by the tabloid press? Yet again there are
subdivisions which reflect the emphasis placed by fans on
different aspects of the Elvis message. The experience of the
Christian church provides a broad parallel. Christians tend to
gather together with other Christians of like mind. Some prefer

forms of worship with a high sacramental content. Others prefer to concentrate on the study of the Word. Others want to be active doing good works in the community. They have no substantial differences of opinion one with another, they just prefer to pursue their faith in the way which is most comfortable and familiar to them. They come together for ecumenical meetings, but by and large tend to go their own way. From time to time there are tensions and arguments. What would appear to outsiders to be small doctrinal differences of opinion are turned into great matters of principle.

This pattern is also followed amongst Elvis fans. A glance at a list of the names chosen by the fan clubs gives some idea of their doctrinal preferences. If it can be argued that the lyrics of the songs recorded by Elvis reflect different aspects of his "message", so it can be said that the choice of name by fans for their club reflects their particular interests.

There is *The Blue Hawaiians Fan Club* in California; *The Elvis Teddy Bears* in Florida; *The Suspicious Minds Fan Club* in Tennessee as well as two clubs in Virginia named after the record *Return to Sender*. *The Elvis Presley Burning Love Fan Club* in Illinois is the club which is much involved in arranging the Graceland anniversary pilgrimages. Other names include, *Elvis Lives On*, *Elvisly Yours*, *Elvis Echoes of Love*, *TCB for Elvis Fans*, *We Remember Elvis Fan Club*, *King of Our Hearts Elvis Presley Fan Club*, *Eternally Elvis*, *Elvis is King Fan Club*, and *The Strictly Elvis Fan Club*. This last name is reminiscent of names taken by some of the exclusive Protestant sects, like the "Strict and Peculiar Baptists". The memory of Elvis is to be strictly adhered to, with no deviations in the direction of The Beatles, Buddy Holly or, perish the thought, Cliff Richard. Indeed, the founders of the club admit to listening to nothing but Elvis music at home or in their car. And then, suggesting a certain rivalry in the ranks, perhaps, there is *The Official Elvis Presley Fan Club of Great Britain*. Like denominations found in other religious movements, the *Official Elvis Presley Fan Club*, claims to derive a special authority to represent the memory of Elvis here on earth from its direct contact with the early disciples. It is run by Todd Slaughter from Leicester and claims to have been started with the authority and approval of Elvis and the Colonel in February 1957. Its magazine, *Elvis Monthly*, claims a readership of 30,000; the worldwide membership is said to be 20,000 fans. The club boasts fifty branches, each of which organises monthly social events, regional conventions and transportation of fans to the many national and international events.

In the third quarter issue of *Graceland Express* in 1991, an article appeared reviewing the club's first thirty-five years. "It was in 1972 that the fan club first took members to see Elvis in cabaret . . . initially these visits each August were arranged to coincide with Presley's annual appearances at the Las Vegas Hilton and continued until 1977." Members were present at Elvis's last concert appearances in 1977 at Cincinnati and Indianapolis. Since Elvis's death members of *The Elvis Presley Fan Club* have returned to Memphis every August and more recently have taken part in the events organised by other fan clubs and the Presley estate. In twenty years the club has taken 10,000 members across the Atlantic, and on the tenth anniversary of his death the official club arranged transport for 1,200 members to visit Graceland.

This year, 1,000 fans will take part in an international meeting in Bad Nauheim, the German town where Presley lived during the time he spent in the American Army in 1959/60; August sees the annual "memorial tour" to Memphis . . . and Tupelo.

In recent years the club has operated "long-weekend" trips to Memphis for fans who cannot afford the time, or perhaps the cost of the two-week-long visits operated in the summer. These are very popular and we have taken up to 300 fans each year.

Our activities are not only confined to holidays overseas. Each year the fan club organises annual charity conventions, and in recent years the club has raised in excess of £100,000 for various good causes.

For fans who cannot afford overseas holidays, the club has operated for the past decade a week long member's holiday at one of Pontin's Holiday Centres. Up to 2,000 fans gather for a week-long thrash of parties, movies, cabaret and other entertainments.

For all the claims that the different Elvis denominations, or fan clubs, live in harmony together, evidence of rivalries emerges from time to time. This was said by an American correspondent to *Elvis World*, estimated readership 20,000 fans, about Todd Slaughter of the *Official Elvis Presley Fan Club of Great Britain*. "While I did not tell Todd I hoped his soul rotted in hell, as I am sure many would have liked for me to have done, I did at least let him know the US fans did not need him to tell them how to run their clubs. I also told him I, for one, had never appointed him to speak for me, which he presumes to do for 'all' Elvis fans." The editor added a note to say that correspondent Pat Geiger of Vermont had sent one of the nicer reactions. "Most were unprintable or the fan club presidents making them asked not to be printed, but did want to get their feelings aired, at least in private!"

So what had Todd Slaughter said? He had complained about the commercialism of Graceland, that it had become a tourist trap, and the inactivity of the fan clubs in the USA.

The fan clubs in the States have been directing all their energies for the last few years in keeping the eternal flame burning at Elvis Presley's grave; complaining and petitioning for postage stamps to be released of Elvis; and slagging off on Priscilla, and more recently Lisa Presley.

Really, Elvis fans are interested in the music and films of Elvis and not interested in the politics.

He said more recently of the American fan clubs that they were small, localized and hated each other.

Neither has there been a totally harmonious relationship between the main British fan clubs. Todd Slaughter and Sid

Shaw have argued over who, to put it in religious terms, represents the true lineage of Elvis. Sid Shaw runs a fan club which he set up in 1984. It is certainly the younger of the two rival clubs, but it came into being, Sid says, to promote harmony between all Elvis followers.

Sid Shaw was also involved in a legal dispute with Graceland over the marketing of souvenirs in Britain. The case went to court, dragged on for years, and Sid lost. It was not, however, a clearcut victory by the Elvis Presley estate and the rights and wrongs of the case were never fully examined, but the complexities of the American legal system proved too much for Sid to fight.

Aware of the tensions in Elvisdom, a fan from Derbyshire recently wrote to *Elvisly Yours* prompted by the need, as he put it, to further the unity of a fandom already second to none. If all branches, he wrote, "now pull together instead of going their own separate ways, the unity we've all been searching for could be just around the corner."

From time to time Elvis fans are admonished for back-sliding. When economic times were tough for many people in the early 1980s in Britain, Sid Shaw's *Elvisly Yours* magazine editorial took some fans to task. It had been noted that fewer fans were making it to the events and fewer requests were being made to radio stations for Elvis records. "For the first time ever I feel fans are slowly forgetting Elvis . . . so get off your backside and start to be true Elvis fans supporting us and every Elvis Club or Association." The temporary dip in Elvis's popularity produced one interesting line in the same editorial. "Readers may be pleased to hear that after writing again to Todd Slaughter he has agreed to meet me to discuss a more harmonious understanding with more unity in the Elvis world." As with all religions, the tendency towards division is only checked when the various denominations start to feel that their individual survival might be threatened by a weakening of the whole.

Whatever internal divisions there might be, there is one thing which can guarantee unanimity – an attack from outside.

Muslims spoke with one voice in condemning the book *The Satanic Verses* for its alleged blasphemy. Huge divisions might have remained as to what to do with the author, but the feeling of revulsion at the slur against the holy prophet was universal. So it is in Elvisdom. All fans hate to hear their King attacked and a gross slander is considered almost as a blasphemy. While some fan clubs grieve in private, others take a more militant line. *Elvis Memphis Style* is a new fan club based in Elvis's home city. Soon after its formation it found itself at the centre of row in which it felt it had a duty to defend the memory of Elvis Presley against what members saw as an outrageous slur. In religious terms they felt called to root out a blasphemy.

It all started as a Hallowe'en joke in October 1991. But it was a joke which badly misfired on its originators, the young person's charitable fund-raising organization, The Greater Mid-South Jaycees. Nationally the Jaycees are a highly respected organization and twenty years ago it honoured Elvis Presley by naming him as one of the Outstanding Young Men of America. Elvis and Priscilla attended a prayer breakfast to receive the award. It was the only award, fans claim, that he ever received in person.

In 1991, fourteen years after the singer's death, the Jaycees constructed a haunted house in Overton Square in Memphis as a fund-raising gimmick and charged people $4 a head to look round. The main feature of the house was the dead Elvis exhibit. The city newspaper *The Commercial Appeal* described what was on show. It horrified the Elvis fans. "A man in Elvis Presley mask and jump suit sat in a coffin thanking visitors for supporting the Jaycees. Empty pizza boxes, pill bottles, half-eaten jelly donuts and a toilet littered the floor of a cobwebbed room. Elvis died in a bathroom."

When news of the exhibit reached the Elvis fans, the Jaycees were bombarded with complaints. Jean Donovan, who had herself moved to Memphis to live just round the corner from Graceland to be near to the Elvis meditation garden, wrote on behalf of the *Elvis Memphis Style* group. She described the exhibit as insulting and demeaning to the memory of an individual who loved Memphis and made it his home.

His admirers come to Memphis in droves. These are family people. There are no drugs, no public drinking, no rowdiness. During his lifetime Elvis gave generously to a multitude of Memphis charitable organisations . . . Memphis would not be the city it is today if it were not for Elvis . . . I will never understand why Elvis is the butt of so many truly stupid, crude and inane jokes . . . Instead of making a joke of him, it would be better if members of the Jaycees would study Elvis's life and music. Then possibly you would begin to see what so many others see. Certainly Memphis has been no friend to Elvis."

The president of the *Elvis Memphis Style* club wrote an open letter to all Elvis fan clubs. It started with a note of weariness, as if defending the reputation of Elvis against insult was becoming too common. "Again we are faced with an outrageous and insulting portrayal of Elvis Presley by Memphians . . . and in this case it is just that much more disturbing since the insult is from the Jaycees, an organisation he admired and whose tribute to him for his humanitarian deeds was his prized possession." Cyndi Sylvia concluded the letter with the words, "Keeping our eyes on the goal, working together for Elvis."

One fan, writing to the *Commercial Appeal* editor, called the exhibition tacky and offensive. "Now the Jaycees join the long list of organisations and individuals who take delight in demeaning and ridiculing a man whose life touched (and continues to touch) millions around the world."

In replying to the criticism the Jaycees claimed that the exhibit had originally intended to use the familiarity of Elvis Presley and the unfortunate manner in which he died, as an avenue to convey an anti-drug message. This, however, inflamed the fans further. In a circular to Elvis fan clubs around the world, the Memphis followers accused the Jaycees of trying to turn a despicable, mean-spirited and insulting exhibit into some great anti-drug campaign! "As we are all aware Elvis's drug problem was with prescription drugs. He did not take street drugs as the general public would, for some perverse reason, like to believe." It was a row about taste which no apology would ever truly heal once the initial hurt was felt. As with any case of "blasphemy", those who are hurt feel a humiliation and wounding which they find hard to convey. Why all the fuss about a silly, if rather tasteless, joke. It could be said of Muslims, why all the fuss about the book *The Satanic Verses*? Does not the truth transcend the words of one biased and opinionated writer? But a believer is insulted because the one he or she holds in great reverence is insulted through them.

Sid Shaw of *Elvisly Yours* in London finds it hard to understand why Elvis is so frequently denigrated, as he sees it, in the popular press. "Elvis brought so much happiness to so many people. Yet you pick up the papers week after week and see sad stories about how he faked his death or committed suicide. It's a farce. It must be because he was so famous. And yet his memory will survive for years and years to come."

Following one article trashing Elvis which appeared in the *Sunday Mirror* in 1984, fans threatened to organize a demonstration march to protest against the way the tabloid press constantly denigrated their hero. At least one threat of physical violence has been made by an Elvis fan against the mockers and detractors, in order to defend the honour of the King. It came in the form of a letter from a fan, Joe Barber, in *Elvisly Yours*:

It's bad enough when I walk through town and receive insults from people on Elvis's behalf. Being an Elvis fan, I expect it from other teenagers, but not from other people such as adults! Sometimes I get into fights, but no matter what, I stick up for ELVIS. From now on people, best watch out. If you're looking for trouble you come to the right place, If you're looking for trouble just look right in my face. ELVIS 1957."

Joe was admonished by an editorial note when his letter was printed in *Elvisly Yours*, for his heavy language. Yet the spirit of his letter is reminiscent of militant Christians prepared to stand up and be mocked for Christ. The Elvis message, as gleaned from his films, is the American message. Good guys can use force in a good cause and if provoked. The myth of the film world, too, is that they usually win if it comes to a fight. No wonder a teenager walking the streets in Elvis Presley gear, and identifying with the Elvis image is going to feel he can retaliate physically when mocked. Whether it can be said he has not provoked the opposition by making such a public and conspicuous declaration of his Elvis faith is open to debate.

Whenever the tabloid press indulges in what the fans see as Elvis bashing, it raises a difficult question for them. All fans admit Elvis was not perfect, but should every detail of his life be exposed to public view? The alternative is to treat him as a plaster saint. And if Elvis's appeal to so many is that they can identify with him and the emotions he expresses, then to treat him as a saint is to undermine that appeal. Some fans say that attacks on Elvis strengthen their devotion.

Almost every church expects its followers to do charitable works. The Elvis cult is no exception. During his lifetime Elvis gave to a whole range of local Memphis charities and his giving is recorded at Graceland. It is said he regularly gave $100,000 each Christmas. Today many fans follow his example. They organize fund-raising events for a whole variety of charitable causes. In particular, however, they collect money in his name to take other fans, especially those with disabilities or disadvantages in life, to Graceland. It is a little like Roman Catholic groups raising money to take people to Lourdes.

Some fans, however, express reservations about this type of giving. An Australian fan, Henry Fong, writing to the *Elvisly Yours* magazine recently said that while he thought raising funds to bring handicapped people to Memphis was a good idea, the money could be more wisely used in other ways, and suggested drug rehabilitation centres. "Elvis had a drug problem and he fought against drugs. Before Elvis died he was going to one for help. I myself have helped in church activities such as showing films at the Sydney City Mission (a crisis centre). Please take this into consideration because Elvis saw the needs. He put biblical principles to practice."

Graceland Express is the official newsletter of Elvis Presley Enterprises which runs Graceland. A glance in just one edition quickly confirms the extent to which Elvis fans are involved in all kinds of charity fund-raising. Giving details of Christmas 1991 at Elvis's home, the *Express* gives news of the regular giving by fans to the Memphis Haemophilia Foundation. The provisional diary for the 1992 Elvis week in August has daily mentions of charitable giving. Whether it is the planned gospel music concert or Elvis sock hop, a charity, the *Express* says, will be chosen to benefit.

Page eight of *Graceland Express* has an illustrated article of the example Elvis set as a fund raiser in his home town. In February 1961, the article recalls, Elvis raised $50,000 for thirty-seven different Memphis organisations.

Often Elvis fans do their good deeds on a one-to-one basis. For instance, Linda and Marie first met when in neighbouring hospital beds. They fell into conversation and Marie began to share with Linda her lifelong enthusiasm for Elvis Presley. She told Linda about the great gathering of Elvis fans at Hemsby near Great Yarmouth. Linda said that one day she would like to go, "It sounded so exciting, the atmosphere, the whole event," but explained that as a single parent on a tight budget, it was very unlikely that she could afford to do so. The two friends kept in touch after their time in hospital and one day Marie announced to Linda that she had arranged for her to attend the convention and had booked a chalet for her. "Elvis fans," Marie said later, "are like a big family. If you can help somebody out, that's what you do. Elvis used to do it, help those less well off, and so should we. As fans we do many things in Elvis's name, for the sake of Elvis. Linda wasn't in a position to afford to come and I felt I could help out. She's a friend. She doesn't get a holiday any other time of the year. So this is her week."

This sense of family is echoed by Pam and Aaron Richie, of the *Strictly Elvis Fan Club*. They have contacts from their base in Southampton with a number of other fan clubs around the world. "We are like a family with different branches. We are supporting Elvis, and it doesn't matter who runs the club." The club has a history of regular fund-raising. No huge sums have been collected, but then Pam and Aaron do not mix in affluent circles. Frequently the money has been raised to help other Elvis fans, less well-off than themselves, to realize their dreams. In July 1986 they raised £325 towards sending two disabled Elvis fans from Manchester on a visit to Memphis. A year later they collected £500 to help another disabled fan travel from Northern Ireland to Elvis's home city. In 1989 they found £300 to help a Russian fan embark on a trip to Graceland.

The charity work by Julian Campo, the Elvis impersonator from Chicago, includes fund-raising performances for a children's hospital and the Arthritis Foundation. For Julian it is a fulfilment of a promise he made to God more than thirty-five years ago. As a young boy growing up in Sicily, Julian, despite frequent illness, dreamed of being a famous singer. He promised God that should one day he be granted his wish he would dedicate his talent to helping others.

"Elvis fans," says Marie, "do a lot of good in Elvis's name. You see the bad things in the papers. Never the good things. We do a great deal for charity. This year we raised £2,500 for children in need." Kiki Apostolakos says that many people who are devoted to Elvis give to charity, but keep their gifts secret. They give, she explains, as a mark of gratitude. They are thankful for his life and example, but they give in the name of Jesus, "because Jesus is love. Elvis is love, too, and if you love Jesus you love Elvis too. If you don't love Jesus you can't love Elvis."

The city of Elvis is of course Memphis, Tennessee, in the new world. But the holiest city of the old world is without doubt Jerusalem. It is the city where three great religious faiths converge. It is the holy city of the Jewish faith, it contains one of the holiest sites in Islam and is of course the holy land for Christians, the city where Christ both died and was raised up from the dead. It is a place of pilgrimage for many millions and to the Jews, part of the promised land. And now it even has a connection with Elvis. On a hill just outside Jerusalem there is now to be found, what is claimed to be the world's largest statue of Elvis Presley. It is twenty feet tall and stands outside the Elvis Inn at Abu Gosh. The statue was placed there by the inn's proprietor, who is a dedicated Elvis fan.

ELEVEN

☆

Shrines and Gatherings

Is it a shop, or is it a warehouse? Visiting fans stopping outside the *Elvisly Yours* headquarters in Shoreditch High Street in the east end of London are not quite sure. It has a shabby front facing a busy city road and yet, to followers of Elvis, the various images of the King of Rock and Roll in the window promise much. To enter you have to press the bell and wait. After a short while someone opens the door, perhaps the owner Sid Shaw himself. You enter a shop with racks of Elvis magazines and souvenirs around. But dominating the whole room is the "shrine". For around the statue of Elvis, which appears larger than life in one corner of the shop, is a pile of cards and letters, messages and flowers meant for Elvis.

The statue, by sculptor Jon Douglas, has found a home at Sid Shaw's *Elvisly Yours* centre after touring Britain's local radio stations and failing to find a permanent place at one of the country's leading museums. It now serves as a focus of adoration for British fans. Followers of Elvis often like to pose for a photograph standing alongside.

Behind the scenes at *Elvisly Yours* is a busy packing department. Mugs, badges, magazines and a whole array of Elvis merchandise is stored and packed to be sent out to fans around the world. Every edition of the *Elvisly Yours* magazine is a mail order catalogue for fans to buy almost anything with an Elvis connection. The Elvisly Yours Centre was opened in

1983 by Jerry and Myrna Schilling. Jerry had been one of Elvis Presley's bodyguards from 1964 to 1976, having met the singer when playing football. Jerry's martial arts nickname was "The Cougar". Jerry and his wife were invited to Britain to open the centre and many other people similarly associated with Elvis have had invitations to visit British fans. These include George Klein, Elvis's friend from his school days in Memphis, and his step-mother Dee Presley. There exists an interesting symbiotic relationship between the fans, on the one hand, and those who knew Elvis, on the other. For the associates of Elvis at meetings with fans, they can enjoy basking in a reflected glory; for the fans, they can thrill and marvel at the idea of shaking the hand that once shook the hand of Elvis.

What is sent out by the Sid Shaw team as one of a consignment, arrives at the home of a fan as a single, eagerly awaited package: the new Elvis plate, the reproduction of a familiar picture as a new poster, the missing edition from a set of magazines, a piece of TCB jewellery. Many of the items Sid imports, buys and provides are destined for the small corners in fans' homes reserved for Elvis. Some devotees plaster the whole house with images of the King, others are more discreet. But thousands of true followers treasure a collection of seemingly ordinary and valueless items which to them are priceless, because of the way these simple objects remind them of Elvis.

Linda has dedicated a corner of her living room to Elvis. There she has put her pictures of Elvis and it is to that alcove she will retreat when she wants to play his music and think about him. "It is as if he is singing personally to me. He has such feeling and emotion."

As early as 1957 there were reports appearing in fan magazines of the dedication of the Davolt sisters from Memphis who had 1,087 pictures of Elvis on their bedroom wall.

Pam and Aaron's home contains a small model of Graceland, which looks very much like a Christmas crib in shape and design, which they decorate at Christmas with cotton wool. They also have a carefully preserved leaf from a tree growing on the Graceland estate.

The minister of a church in Memphis tells the story of a member of his congregation who had an Elvis room at her home. It was decorated with pictures of the singer and memorabilia from Graceland. She would go into the room and talk to Elvis. The minister was concerned about the amount of time and energy that went into this exhibition of devotion, but accepted that there was little he could do except, in his words, "point out that the presence of God was more real than the presence of Elvis."

Did the woman involved see any contradiction between her talking to Elvis in the shrine room and her professed belief in Christ? "Not this lady, her belief in Christ was so shallow. She had placed Christ in a box. For everyone else there was a contradiction, but not for her. Elvis was more real to her than Christ, by her choice."

And a further illustration taken from a typical fan magazine letter, "I have been a fan of Elvis for years . . . I have posters, photos and small mementoes in my bedroom and listen to Elvis music nearly every week, so you see Elvis is much alive. Some day I would love to go to Memphis, maybe in two or three years' time."

Both fans who have never been to Memphis and those who know Memphis well have their "shrines" and special times to remember Elvis. Dorothy Smith, who spent hours at Graceland the day Elvis died, and who was one of the fans who viewed his body, frequently sets time aside to brings Elvis to mind. She watches his films and listens to records and tapes and would never, she says, be parted from his *Moody Blue* album, whatever sum of money she was offered. *Moody Blue* was recorded in 1976, much of it at Graceland, and released in July 1977, just before Elvis's death.

Dorothy's most treasured possession of Elvis must surely be her memories of the day of his death and the hours which followed when she was one of the few to see his body before the funeral. But like many other Elvis fans she also has her mementoes at home.

I have clippings, writings, pictures, pretty well what everybody's got, I've got some of it too. I still feel the spirit of Elvis. A lot of people might think it's silly. Memphis to me is Elvis. I feel his spirit almost physically. When I see him on a movie, I think if I could just touch him. I fantasize about seeing him in person. I don't want to harm him, just want to touch him. He's so real. I drift with his music, he was great and I think he's in heaven. Some people say he isn't really dead, he's hid somewhere, but I don't believe that. He's dead, in heaven. It's tragic, he had such a good life ahead of him. I don't go as far as praying to Elvis, I just hate it that he's gone and had to die so young. He was just a year older than me.

I went to a concert, which was more than a lot of people did. When I listen to his music I like to be alone so that I can cry. My children understand and leave me be. They know how I am. I am serious about him.

For a true Elvis fan to live in a house without a single memento of Elvis on show would be like a devout Roman Catholic keeping all images of Christ, Mary and the saints out of view. In 1984 a woman from Wakefield in Yorkshire wrote to a fan magazine. She began her letter by saying that she had three children, her husband was unemployed and they relied on social security benefits in their various forms to live. She continued, "real fans do need Elvis items around their houses." Those who feel they can get on without, she claimed were not real fans. "Believe me, I have love in my heart for Elvis. I am proud to be an Elvis fan and by having him around my house I feel that I am giving my children the best example I ever could."

Long before Christians built churches, the faithful gathered for worship in each others homes or in halls hired for the occasion. Indeed, today there is a growing movement amongst certain Christians to return to the practices of the first followers of Jesus, and the house church movement is growing rapidly. Elvis fans, too, meet together in each others homes to mark anniversaries and to listen to Elvis music and talk about the

King. Pam and Aaron Richie invite fellow fans round on the anniversary of Elvis's death to play his music, watch his videos and talk of him "in the past and in the present". Younger Elvis fans are welcomed and the older ones talk about how they came to know Elvis. It is not a sad occasion, says Pam. "But it is no party, just a get together. Fans want to be with other fans on that particular day. Sometime between half past nine and ten in the evening, the equivalent time here to the time when Elvis's death was announced in Memphis, we have a time of silence. Members of the fan club appreciate that."

"I get a tear in my eye," says Aaron. "I tighten up inside. But it's not a sad occasion, nor a happy occasion. It is the time to be together with other fans on a special day. I don't feel Elvis's presence specially, as I feel he is with me always."

The birthday celebration in January follows much the same pattern. If August is the Good Friday in the Elvis calendar, 8 January is the Christmas. "We have a party," says Aaron, "we cut a cake, have a disco and a chat about all things Elvis." Sometimes they talk with friends about Elvis for eight or more hours.

Sometimes larger meetings are organized. A glance through any British fan magazine provides a choice of places to go to remember Elvis. In Hitchin in Hertfordshire regular Elvis shows are held throughout the year, sometimes two a month. Elvis weekends are held at a hotel in Blackpool where live groups, discos, films, quizzes and Elvis competitions are arranged for fans at prices ranging from £59 upwards.

In 1985, the year Elvis would have been fifty had he lived, August was a specially busy time for Elvis fans. In Britain alone there were many major events in centres such as Gloucester, Birkenhead, Newcastle, Peterborough, Nottingham and in Scotland. Some events were special film shows, others took the form of discos or tributes by Elvis impersonators. In London the Elvisly Yours Centre was open all day on the sixteenth to receive flowers and wreaths from fans, which were placed at the foot of the Elvis statue.

To some events special speakers might be invited, people

who knew Elvis or have a special knowledge of him. A line in a recent fan magazine illustrates this well, "Elvis's aunt Rev Nash Pritchett, and Eddie Fadal will speak at Alice Schlichte's Elvis Lives On Campaign convention on Sept. 9 at Nendel's Motor Inn in Tukwila, WA." Eddie Fadal was a radio disc jockey and early friend of Elvis, and Nash Pritchett (née Presley) was Vernon's sister.

Without doubt gatherings of Elvis fans are extra special if, as guest of honour, the fans can invite someone who met or knew the King. In and around Memphis this is not difficult to arrange, but for fans thousands of miles away a visit by such a person is a major event. One can imagine, to draw a parallel, the meetings of early Christians in the first century. For most of the time they met in each others houses for worship and practised their faith in isolation. Then news would come that one of the apostles was journeying in their part of the world. He would bring not only the direct testimony of a man who heard the words of Christ, but someone who had touched him, eaten with him, travelled with him. For all the inner conviction in each believer that Christ was alive and with them always, the physical contact would have produced a special excitement. So it is with Elvis's fans and one of the pulls of Graceland is that it provides fans with the tangible evidence of Elvis's life. There, too, they can meet people who saw Elvis, spoke to Elvis, possibly are even family relations of Elvis.

In Britain, the major events for the Elvis fans, whether or not a special guest is expected, are the conventions. The annual Elvis get-together at the holiday camp at Hemsby is a week in the year every British fan longs for and saves to get to. In the ballroom, dining areas and chalets, the talk is nothing but Elvis. There is a special Elvis television channel organized so that fans can keep in touch wherever they are in the holiday centre.

At conventions the fans have actions and movements to accompany songs. It is as if a huge hall of people is participating in some ritual dance. The music is inevitably brought to a climax with the singing of the *American Trilogy* and as the words, "Glory, glory, alleluia," are chanted from the famous battle-hymn, fans hold their hands in the air as if delegates at an evangelical Christian convention.

The climax of the gathering is a moment of great emotion. After the hours of dancing and entertainment and meeting with old friends, all the Elvis fans are gathered in the ballroom of the holiday camp. The compere attracts the attention of, perhaps, 1,500 people in the darkened hall and slowly counts down from five. The hubbub in the room fades as the countdown continues, "Four" . . . "Three" . . . Even the area around the bar becomes unusually hushed . . . "Two" . . . "One". The minute's silence for Elvis starts. Linda describes the effect:

> It really is uncanny. The reason we are all down here is to show our respect. But the room goes absolutely quiet. People have been drinking, all day some of them, but as the countdown ends you could hear a pin drop. It's incredible, so emotional.
>
> Elvis is there. You can feel him. He is around us all the time. You feel him in you. I wish he was here in person, in the flesh. We just have to do what we do and think about him. We keep him alive by what we are doing.
>
> The first year I came and the silence was held, I couldn't believe it was happening. It was so incredible. I get a lump in my throat just thinking about it. It was an uncanny feeling. There were 1,500 people in the hall and they had been dancing and drinking, but as soon as the man at the microphone called for silence and reminded us all that we were there for one man and one man only, Elvis, it all went so hushed.

When a religion is truly established, it is no longer sufficient to borrow halls or holiday camps to meet for worship, and homes are far too small. Followers begin to build churches and temples. The holy city, the place from which the faith moved out into the world, also needs a substantial shrine or temple.

Rome has St Peter's; Jerusalem has the Dome of the Rock, the Church of the Holy Sepulchre and the Wailing Wall, the remains of the Jewish temple. This is the stage usually when the secular authorities begin to muscle in. They too want to be seen to be in line with the truth. Perhaps they also feel the need to claim for themselves some divine authority. And so it is, one could argue, in the case of Elvis. Alongside the great wide river Mississippi at Memphis, near the unromantically named Mud Island, the city has built a huge monument to itself, a massive pyramid of steel and reflective glass, the realised dream of the city mayor, an old friend of Elvis. Not surprisingly the city's most famous son is honoured inside. For the pyramid not only contains a huge stadium, but also exhibitions, including a whole section on rock 'n' roll. Since the time of the Egyptian pharaohs, it has been claimed that pyramids have magical and mysterious properties. The citizens of Memphis hope that their great modern temple will attract visitors in their thousands, especially those who first come to Memphis to visit Graceland.

More sharply focused Elvis "cathedrals" are being planned, and not just in America. Imagine this scene in a few years time.

A huge sign in both English and Japanese greets the orderly lines of visitors: "Welcome to Elvistown". Then, as they enter the site itself, their excitement mounts. There, in front of their eyes, is America. But this is Japan! The visitors have stepped out of their own culture into another, the one they see on the films and hear about on the pop records. The small American town with its drive-in restaurant, movie palace, record store, court house, bank and fifties shops might all be a Disneyland-style sham, but the people are real. Shopkeepers, cops, youngsters in authentic replica fifties outfits, walk the streets. And the music is real. Elvis records blast out from the jukeboxes.

All this is, as yet, in the planning stage, but by 1994 it is hoped to have built an Elvis shrine in Japan. It will be the world's biggest and most lavish Elvis shrine outside Graceland. The business brains behind the Elvis estate are of the opinion that Japan is going though the social, cultural and economic changes America experienced in the fifties. Consequently there will be a growing interest in Japan in the idea of the American dream. They feel the America dream has a universal appeal and Elvis sang the music, drove the big cars, dated the women, had the clothes, style, fame and fortune, indeed epitomizes the whole concept.

Knowing the Japanese ability to adopt and adapt cultures from around the world, it is felt that a Japanese Elvis shrine will attract thousands of visitors. And thousands of visitors means millions of yen. It will be a project which will go some way towards righting the imbalance of trade between the two countries. As Japan grows in economic strength, America will start to market its "heritage", in much the way that the British market their history to the Americans today.

From the Elvistown plot, the visitors will go to the Elvis museum and audio-visual centre, where all the latest electronic techniques will be used to bring the Elvis legend alive. In addition, real Elvisana from the Graceland stores and closets will be on show. The Japanese Elvis fans will be able to see the costumes he wore on stage and the day-to-day objects he used and handled in life. Little mention will be made of the dark side of the Elvis story. All will be upbeat, carefully packaged and designed to please and inspire the true Elvis fans, interest the general visitor and persuade both categories to part with their money at the souvenir shops.

If Elvistown, Japanese style, succeeds, other Elvistowns could follow. There could be one in Britain or continental Europe, in a number of American cities, even perhaps one across the road from Graceland in Memphis. There the idealised Elvis home town set could be created. It would be sheer nostalgic indulgence, with little resemblance to reality, other than the "reality" of the world Elvis had created for him in his films. And even before Elvistowns spring up around the world, plans are afoot for a new travelling museum to take to the road and the air, bringing the Elvis message to fans around America and the world.

Once a church or denomination begins to grow, it starts to build. It is not simply a question of size, that homes and hired halls can no longer take the numbers of devotees who wish to meet, it is a question of dedication. To build a temple, shrine, church or cathedral, is an act of worship in itself. The best craftsmen and artists are employed and the whole structure, it is said, is built to the glory of God. In the case of the Elvistown projects, commercial interests are providing a significant impetus. But to the true Elvis fan, a visit to an Elvistown could provide a special experience. Without needing to travel to Graceland, it will be possible to get close to Elvis and to drink in the atmosphere of his time and indulge in the spirit of his age.

Only time will tell if the structures built to honour Elvis acquire a special mystique.

☆

TWELVE

For Ever Elvis?

Two famous quotes are attributed to Sam Phillips, the record producer who first recognized the potential in the Elvis image and sound.

The first predates his meeting with the gauche Memphis teenager. "If I could find a white man who had the negro sound and the negro feel, I could make a billion dollars."

The second was uttered much later when Elvis was a proven international megastar. "I knew Elvis was going to be big, but I never knew he'd be that big!"

To these two quotes, a third must now be added. In 1982 Sam Phillips is reported as having told a gathering of fans in Memphis, "The two most important events in American history were the birth of Jesus and the birth of Elvis Presley."

There is no formal way of showing that interest in Elvis is on the increase, but there is certainly plenty of anecdotal evidence which points in that direction and suggests why the growth is taking place. One person well situated to form an opinion is Harold Loyd, Elvis's cousin. Not only does he meet many visitors as they arrive at Graceland, he also has a network of contacts with fans around the world. He has been the guest of Elvis fans in Britain and hears from many who like to be in touch with one of Elvis's family.

I always knew he had talent, but I never dreamed he would

ever be this big. Fifteen years after he died he is still popular and that popularity is growing. I have talked to a lot of people since his death who told me they weren't Elvis fans when he was alive, but after hearing all the critics they came to his defence, and they became Elvis fans because of that.

Elvis could never understand what he had done or was doing to deserve all the fame. I remember him once when he was in the house looking at a television monitor showing all the crowds at the gate. "I guess I'll never understand," he said, "but I must be doing something they like. They keep coming back." But he wouldn't dwell on the subject. I am sure he never could understand.

And even more difficult to comprehend is the fact that today the Elvis message is reaching a generation which never knew the King alive. Some Elvis fans were not born in 1977. Diane Brown at the Elvis centre in Tupelo has noticed the increasing numbers of new, young fans coming to his birthplace. They have been attracted, she says, by his records and the television programmes of his concerts they have seen of him. The Elvis Youth Page in *Elvis World* resembles the pages in certain religious publications which list birthdays, baptisms or barmitzvahs.

"I am eleven years old. I have been an Elvis fan since I was six," says John Paul.

"My earliest recollection of being an Elvis fan was when I was five," says Kelly. "I think it is every young Elvis fan's dream to have been able to see him live in concert. We are just lucky enough that we are able to see Elvis on video."

"Dustin is five and must be one of the youngest Elvis fans around," writes his proud Uncle Michael. "His favourite songs are *Blue Suede Shoes*, *Teddy Bear* and *Hound Dog*. He has been a fan since he was three. He cuts Elvis pictures out of all magazines and puts them on the wall. I guess it is never too early (or too late, for that matter) to become an Elvis fan."

One explanation is that although, by the standards of many religions, the Elvis phenomenon is still very young, there are already instances of the faith being handed on from parents to children. One case in point is that of the Elvis impersonator Louie Michael Bunch Junior. He was only six years old when Elvis Presley died, but was nevertheless an established fan. He remembers the day clearly because everyone around him in his family was so upset by the news.

Jeffrey Marn was even younger when he started out as an impersonator, and at the age of ten appeared on national television in the United States. He too was a "cradle Elvis fan", having been captured by the Elvis sound and image after watching one of his aunt's videos.

The big day for dressing up in America is Hallowe'en when children put on fancy costumes to go to parties or terrorize the neighbourhood with their demands of "trick or treat". In the past children dressed up as witches and ghosts, but more recently they have turned to a whole range of other ideas, dressing as television or film stars. Not suprisingly the children of Elvis fans often ask and are encouraged to dress as Elvis. Hair is blackened and slicked back. Sideburns are pasted on and the sons and daughters squeezed into home-sewn jumpsuits. Then with guitar in hand they are ready.

There are other occasions for dressing up, and sometimes a young son in tow as the parents visit Graceland is dressed as a mini-Elvis. A well practised mini-Elvis comes complete with curled lip and a repertoire of poses. Children dressed as Elvis are adored and indulged by adult audiences when they appear at conventions and look-alike competitions. For in some ways the Elvis cult is about eternal youth. It does not promise that the devotee will avoid the trials and tribulations of the physical ageing process. But it does suggest that Elvis followers will remain for ever young in mind. Elvis will never be an old man. Therefore, whatever a fan's physical age or state, to be like Elvis, to live like Elvis, is to become and remain the eternal child. And many reports of his life indeed suggest that a great part of the Elvis character was that of the child. He was devoted to his mother and reacted to her death with an uncontrollable grief. He retained a sense of wonder, awe and delight. He enjoyed visiting the amusement park in Memphis and would sometimes hire the entire show for himself and friends and would spend hours riding the dodgems and other attractions. He pigged on junk food. He had a naive dependence on his manager, who treated him as an adult might treat a child. He had the short attention span of a child and the tantrums of a spoiled brat if he could not get his way. But at the same time he had many of the endearing qualities of a child. This was part of his secret as an entertainer. Women talk of their maternal feelings towards him when he was alive, and, after death, of the continuing urge to protect him from others and himself.

Inevitably there are fans who find that in remembering Elvis and keeping his memory alive, they are keeping alive that period of their own lives when they were young, and life was full of hope and promise. Fans who are now in their fifties, the age Elvis would be if still alive, lived through a period of great upheaval in popular music and American culture. Elvis inspired them to be part of the great cultural changes of their time. It was the time when youth culture began to be noticed, when the word teenager entered the vocabulary. In the fifties young people began to feel important. Elvis led the way. And today the same fans, now stuck in middle age, with middle incomes and little hope now of achieving great things in life, can return inside themselves to times past, and Elvis leads the way again.

Fans who are shy about announcing their interest in and devotion to Elvis spread the message quietly. It travels by word of mouth from friend to friend, despite the fact that, in the main, the media does little to help the process of Elvis evangelism. Fans continually complain that all the newspapers want to do is publish the latest off-beat stories about Elvis being sighted, or recycle old scandal. Fans also say the broadcast media do little to promote Elvis. National pop stations like Britain's BBC Radio I, they say, are only interested in the play lists of the week and the current charts. Television programmes on Elvis too are rare, considering the degree of interest and the size of the potential audience. It has to be pointed out that a major American network Elvis show "bombed", but who can tell if this was because of the subject or the treatment.

Some Elvis fans talk of those who have not yet found Elvis as "being on the outside". Those who come to occasional gatherings, or profess to like his music, but not be dedicated to the memory of the man, are "on the border". Pam Richie says many people are held back from declaring their 100% devotion to Elvis by what friends might think. She also feels it important to hand on their knowledge of Elvis to a new generation and with her husband has a willing pupil in a local teenager who visits them and plies them with questions about their hero.

There have been some dramatic conversions. Harold Loyd tells of one involving a young woman who has now been a dedicated Elvis follower for four years. Her mother was an Elvis fan and yet for years her daughter showed no interest. She would encourage her daughter to listen to Elvis's music and call her to see him when he appeared on the television. Yet to no avail. Her daughter showed no interest. Until one day, she saw Elvis on the television and, says Harold, instantly became a fan. Why then and so suddenly cannot be explained. Today she is one of the King's most ardent followers.

Alongside the stories of dramatic conversions in most religions, are the stories of dramatic healing, although as yet there has been no flood of reports. One interesting incident, however, concerns a woman from Hemel Hempstead in Hertfordshire, who, in her mid-forties had a bad accident at work. She had always loved Elvis and when in pain from the accident, she says, she turned to the King and played his records. After being confined to a wheel-chair for two years she suddenly found she could walk, dance and run, just as she had before the accident.

Many Elvis fans are enthusiastically evangelistic, wanting to spread the word of their discovery of Elvis to anyone who will listen. Recruiting literature comes, inevitably, in all shapes and designs. The sheet sent out by *The Elvis Presley Burning Love Fan Club* is typical in that it is an inexpensive single sheet of pink/orange A4 paper printed on both sides. On the one side is a picture of the mature Elvis under the two words in capital letters, "BURNING LOVE". The reverse gives the address of the club, the name of its president, Bill De Night, of Streamwood, Illinois, and the Eternal President, Elvis Presley. Membership is offered to US fans at $12 a year and overseas fans at $15. "This fan club is built entirely out of and on the love we share for the greatest entertainer that ever lived, Elvis Presley. Join us in helping keep his memory alive *forever!*" Membership benefits listed are being sent four newsletters a year accompanied by a photograph of Elvis, a membership card, a photo button and another picture of the King of Rock and Roll. The club states that it is a non-profit organization which supports various charities in Elvis's name. And the invitation to join ends with the words, "We sincerely hope that you will enjoy sharing 'the love of Elvis' with us."

There is nothing flash about the membership form. Very few fan clubs have many funds as most are made up of ordinary people living on modest incomes. The Elvis cult may have a quasi-religious feel to it, but unlike many cults around today, indeed unlike many evangelical Christian ministries, it is not involved in a permanent drive for donations. There is a thriving, but not large, trade in relatively inexpensive mementoes, but there is no Elvis TV evangelist making a name and a living from telling fans to tithe or give generously for the good of their souls and for the greater glory of Elvis.

A new Elvis recruit, captivated by the music and the image, may in time start delving more deeply into the world and mind of the King.

There is the interest amongst many fans to look for parallels between the life of Jesus and that of Elvis, but do they equate the two figures in their minds? One possible litmus test is to ask, do Elvis fans risk persecution and martyrdom? Elvis fans have not yet been stoned to death or executed on an upturned cross, but they do risk being mocked and in some countries fans have been subjected to severe political disapproval.

When the Elvis story reached the old Soviet bloc in the darker days of communism, Elvis fans reportedly suffered some of the same experiences suffered by Christians who deviated from what was permitted. In the days of the Soviet Union, before glasnost heralded the momentous changes of the last few years, Elvis music was only heard by devotees who could tune in to international radio stations or who could find means of buying, or borrowing, smuggled tapes. As few of the international radio broadcasts carried Elvis music, and at times many stations from the decadent West were jammed, illegal recordings were the only way of keeping in regular touch with the message of the King. Nevertheless, the Elvis sound was known about and there were even secret meetings of fans who gathered together to share their information, in the way that dissident Christian groups met at dead of night in obscure forest clearings. When in 1990 the American Elvis impersonator Jerome Marion visited Moscow, Leningrad and Krasnodar, he was not sure what to expect. Did the citizens from the countries which were once hidden by the iron curtain know anything about Elvis? Would they appreciate his music? He performed at youth camps and was amazed at the enthusiasm of the welcome and the knowledge the young people of Russia had of the King of Rock and Roll.

Elvis Presley first came to prominence at the height of the Cold War and the first Elvis records were not heard in the USSR until 1958 when *Jailhouse Rock* was smuggled across the iron curtain and rerecorded secretly on to old X-ray plates. The plates were still showing images of broken bones and so the rock and roll music became known as "music on the bones". According to Sid Shaw, who runs the *Elvisly Yours* business selling Elvis souvenirs,

> When rock and roll was in effect illegal, many artists were put in prison. There was a law in the sixties which said that any music group could only have one guitar. Music was available on the black market, and to be caught trading on the black market was illegal. The recordings available were of very bad quality as they had been copied over and over

again to pass them round. If concerts were held the authorities would harass the performers. Lights would be turned off, musicians arrested and gaoled until the audience dispersed.

An ironic twist to the Russian experience came about after the fall of the Berlin Wall, when a leading Russian Elvis impersonator sought to visit the USA. When Rafik Kashapov applied for a visa to visit Elvis's native land, an iron curtain of bureaucracy barred his way. American consulate officials in Leningrad were convinced Rafik wanted to go to America to work as an entertainer and refused him permission to enter the country. He pleaded with everyone, even sent a message to President Bush. The American dream however remained elusive. By way of some small compensation, Elvis fans commissioned a replica Elvis jumpsuit for Rafik, which together with a replica jewel-studded belt, was presented to the disappointed singer in St Petersburg, or Leningrad as it then was.

Rafik had to wait many more months before his dream to visit America was realised. And even when all the documentation was in order he had problems with officials at the airport on landing. Fortunately one of the officials was herself an Elvis fan and after a considerable delay and no little anxiety, Rafik was allowed to go on his way to Memphis. And before leaving the airport Rafik entertained the assembled officials with an Elvis number.

When communication with the West became open after President Gorbachev took over the leadership of the USSR and introduced a new policy of openness, Elvis fan clubs started receiving letters from Soviet citizens. They asked for penfriends, news, contacts of any sort and slowly a picture built up of the extent of the infiltration of the Elvis message during the grimmer years of communism.

Such was the isolation of many Soviet rock and roll fans that when the Russian Kolya Vasin finally managed to make a journey to the West in 1989 and was offered a drink of Coca

Cola, he had never tasted it before. Kolya has been a devotee of western music, Elvis in particular, since 1958. At that time Elvis was condemned totally by the Communist Party and the Soviet regime as decadent. Kolya is an artist and poet who from one room acts as the main rock and roll contact in his country. He is not an exclusive Elvis fan and likes The Beatles, Little Richard and others, but it was to Graceland he particularly wanted to go when Elvis fans helped find funds to bring him to the West. The money had been raised under the Presleynost banner, a project which stemmed from an idea by Elvis's Aunt Loraine. So when Kolya arrived in The States he was big news. He was living proof of the Cold War thaw of the glasnost era. It was a highly symbolic visit both for Kolya and the American public. To Kolya it was all an amazing dream come true. He was an Elvis fan and had lived, breathed and preached Elvis even during the darkest days of communism. He came as quite an eye-opener to many Americans. The huge political changes in the old communist east have called for many readjustments to be made by the American people. Ideas and simplistic political notions concerning the citizens of the former eastern bloc have had to be jettisoned. The arrival of Kolya has helped many do this. Elvis fans with wider thoughts concerning the ultimate purpose of Elvis's mission on earth, will not have failed to notice Elvis's role in helping Americans come to terms with the new world order, and that it was through an Elvis fan that Americans came to know Soviets as people and not as ogres.

The American media called Kolya Russia's biggest rock and roll fan and television cameras followed his every move. Writing of the event later Sid Shaw said, "Although his English was limited, Kolya made himself understood and brought a spiritual awareness to the whole project. To him, visiting Graceland was a religious experience and he knelt and prayed at Elvis's grave and at the cross which was his mother's memorial."

Sid Shaw estimates that there are between fifty and one hundred thousand Elvis fans in Britain of which around 20,000 are super-dedicated – they decorate their homes with Elvis pictures and are dedicated to his memory. He says the number of fans is increasing and points to the growing number of young fans showing interest in his music.

The memory of Elvis will survive into future centuries. It will last for as long as his music is played. It will reach out over the generations and the years.

He appeals to all types of people. There is something special, magical about his voice. It is very reassuring, very relaxing, very soothing. I know of one lady who was disabled and swears Elvis helped her walk. There was someone else who was feeling so low and depressed that they thought suicide was the only option until hearing Elvis sing the great gospel hymn, *How Great Thou Art*.

In a hundred years time there may well be an Elvis religion. Hopefully this religion will not involve bombs and guns as sadly many religions today are an excuse for hatred. To me Elvis is just happiness.

As one fan wrote in 1982 of her earlier visit to Las Vegas to see Elvis,

Now, when I look back, I thank God I did see Elvis. Every true fan deserved the same privilege as myself and believe me, I feel deeply honoured that I was one of the lucky ones. I can't wait to tell my grandchildren someday . . . "Do you know, your grandmother saw Elvis Presley on stage?" I just know they'll sigh in wonder and envy because all future generations will love Elvis as we do now, after all he will always be the KING!

And so will start an oral tradition to back up the evidence of the tapes. Memories will be embroidered and then petrified as legends. Some time in the middle of the next century, a wizened centenarian will be discovered as the last person still alive who had seen Elvis in the flesh. He or she will recount a well-rehearsed tale and future generations will listen in awe.

How long, though, will Elvis not simply be remembered by a few but continue to have a substantial army of dedicated followers? Jennifer Walker, the British woman who has come to live in Memphis to be near Graceland, does not think that there will be thousands of fans visiting for ever. Things will evolve, she says, "but he will be talked about in the next century. The love is beautiful".

*

The future course of the Elvis cult could be influenced by what happens to the Elvis financial legacy. Soon his only daughter Lisa Marie inherits, and what she chooses, or is advised to do, with her new power and wealth is crucial. In the long term will she want to sell Graceland? Will she be manipulated by advisers, who in turn will seek to manipulate the memory of her father? What if she came under the influence of another religious movement? Perhaps a movement like the Scientologists which has had a controversial history and whose founder L Ron Hubbard has been accused of being a manipulating charlatan and fraud. Priscilla Presley and Lisa have both been reported as showing an interest in Scientology. To date, however much the Elvis movement is seen as a cult, no one has ever accused it of being a dangerous one. It is a cult in that it is, to borrow a dictionary definition, a system of religious devotion, homage to a person or thing. In recent times the term cult has also gathered to it other connotations which are not present in the Elvis movement. There have been no reports of Elvis fans being brainwashed or kept at centres of indoctrination against their will. No parents have yet tried to kidnap, rescue and reprogramme offspring who have been drawn into the movement by sinister Elvis devotees. No one has been forced to worship the King of Rock and Roll by coercion, threats, sleep deprivation or any other illegal or improper means. The fan clubs are not structured into an organization which has a leader who controls the lives of the Elvis followers. Any real danger of these things happening would be if Graceland and the control of the main souvenir businesses came under the control of an individual or organization with ulterior motives.

Amongst the messages written to Elvis on the stone wall at Graceland is one which differs from all the hundreds of others. It, too, is addressed to Elvis, but is it really intended for him or his fans?

"Elvis, please repent and accept Jesus Christ as your Lord and Saviour."

The Elvis cult is beginning to be of concern to Christians. One pastor in Ashford in Kent, for instance, remembers a member of his congregation coming to him and asking for an Elvis corner in the church, a request he did not feel it was appropriate to grant. There have been no reports of Elvis followers being psychologically damaged by their devotion, although some outsiders might judge their behaviour to be odd. But some Christians are concerned that Elvis followers are embracing an erroneous doctrine. There is one way to God and that is through Jesus, they would say, and not Elvis.

Not far from Graceland on Elvis Presley Boulevard in Memphis, there is a thriving Methodist church. It has an active school and generally serves the neighbourhood. The main road itself has few homes, but is mostly lined with fast food establishments, general shops, hotel advertising hoardings and gas station. But off the main road, in the district of Whitehaven, are a number of residential estates. The houses are not lavish, but the area is not poor either. It is solid middle America.

To the minister of the church and the sister Methodist churches in the area, Elvis Presley is a fact of life. He is a tourist attraction and local people are well used to seeing the fans milling around the gates and the souvenir shops. While there are some Memphis fans, most of the fans who come to Graceland are from other states and from overseas. Elvis is big business for the city hotels and eating places. As impartial observers, the local ministers affirm that the number of fans coming each year is appearing to grow. The older, devoted fans are staying devoted, they feel, and there are more and more younger people showing an interest in Elvis.

One of the local Methodist ministers, the Reverend Thomas Bullock, is in no doubt that what he sees of the Elvis fans is a cult.

You hear them talking as if Elvis is still alive and some of them think he is still alive. Others think he is dead, but there are mixed feelings. I have mingled with them a few times during Elvis week and found it amusing and interesting. They get so excited.

I am not sure if it is a "religious" cult. The fans seem to have a lot of devotion for him. In restaurants you hear them talking constantly about Elvis and his generosity, gifts and works of charity.

It is rather pathetic, I think; some individuals who seem to have no purpose in life and are looking for purpose find Elvis and maybe use him as a God. Some of them think of him as a God, judging from their devotion.

The message they find in the cult is perhaps one of hope. That Elvis grew up obscure, poor and seemed to make a big success. If he can do that, them perhaps other people can.

And as if to prove the old saying that a prophet is seldom honoured in his own country, Thomas Bullock adds, "Memphis people in the main like Elvis. He was generous to many charities. There is a trauma centre in the city called after him. But they don't see him as a cult figure. Just as an entertainer, the local boy who made good in the movies and the pop charts." But not all of Thomas Bullock's colleagues would agree with his assessment of the Elvis phenomenon. Others would see the "worship" of Elvis as being in a heroic tradition and play down suggestions of religious overtones. They claim the Elvis followers have none of the rituals of cult membership; even the annual Graceland candlelight vigil is seen as "just the highlight of a vacation" for those who attend.

One of the local ministers now serving in the area knew Elvis. The singer was fascinated with all matters to do with law enforcement and made a particular point of making friends with members of the local police department. Back in the days when Elvis would sometimes hire a whole cinema for himself and invited guests, The Reverend Wesley Fears was not ordained but serving as a Memphis cop. He was sometimes invited to join Elvis at the night-time movie shows. He also met Elvis at a Graceland party and in the sixties had the chance to play football against him. Elvis knocked him down and two plays later Wesley sent the famous rock star flying. He remembers Elvis saying at the time that he wished he had more opportunities to lead a more ordinary life.

I thought he was a very humble, genuine, honest person. Yet he was the kind of person who, when he entered the room, you knew it. He could not sneak into a room. He had tremendous charisma. A gift from God. You see some people who have it and others who don't have it. It is a presence, and he had that gift.

His death was such a shock to my generation that many continue to manifest their adoration for him and to him. This manifestation has a spiritual element only in the fact that it speaks to some people's spirits. Not so much a religious element as a spiritual one.

One of the interesting things about Elvis was that no matter what he did, people seem to always equate him and his life with Christianity, with being a good, decent, God loving, God fearing person. No matter what he did people equate with him those values that are important to them. Even still there are people who do that when they think of Elvis. He espoused family values, loved his family, took care of his family. Money never seemed to rob him of his basic character.

I don't know why they overlook the sad last years, perhaps it's the easiest thing to do. It is almost as if people say that when Priscilla left, Elvis fell apart. I've heard that, maybe, I don't know.

People are not wanting the whole message of Elvis's life, that you can rise from obscurity, gain the whole world and yet that alone will never fully satisfy. People want just part of the message. It is a lot like Christianity. We want part of the message, but not the whole of the message. In Elvis's life, it is the same way. The whole message of Elvis is that our actions and our behaviour have consequences. If you gain the whole world, but lose your soul, it's been fruitless.

Wesley Fears has also considered the idea of Elvis's death being this generation's sacrifice or atonement. He does not accept that Elvis's death has a mystical purpose, but acknowledges it to have been a sacrifice in one sense: his death was a reminder to others of the futility of achieving wordly wealth and fame, if in the process the soul is lost.

In the Old Testament there is a familiar story which tells of the Israelites turning away from God in order to worship a golden calf. The Israelites grew impatient waiting for Moses to return to them from Mount Sinai. They wanted instant results to their prayers for a God to lead them forward. So it was suggested they collect together all their gold and melt it down and make it into a golden image of a bull calf. This they did and when the image was complete they danced around it, feasting and drinking. When Moses returned, in his anger, he ordered that the image be ground to powder and the Israelites mix it in water and drink it. And the man who had encouraged the Israelites to make the calf, the symbol of worldly wealth, was Aaron.

As the minister for the last three years at the church on Elvis Presley Boulevard, the Reverend Charles Leist welcomes visiting Elvis fans to Sunday worship. In August 1991, he even had a request from a couple from Indiana to perform a marriage ceremony at Graceland. At first he had some reservations and called the bride on the telephone and questioned her as to why they wished to be married at Elvis Presley's home.

She was very sincere and said that to have the ceremony there would be very meaningful to her. It was a Christian wedding. I used the service I would have used in my sanctuary. That is what she wanted. She was a devoted Elvis fan and had been for some time. She was very respectful of that. She wanted a wedding in the Elvis setting, but I made no reference to him in the service.

The death of Elvis helped people come into contact with their mortality. The fact that Elvis was a relatively young man when he died has a lot to do with the feelings people have for him now. Had he lived out his life and retired after another fifteen or twenty years, I don't know if he would have had the same impact. But his death coming at the time that it did, people have some guilt themselves about his death. They wish that it could have been different. That they could have done something to prolong his life. This happens when well-known people die young. People wish things could have been different and wonder if they could have had a part in making things different. To make up for that guilt they continue to come and pay tribute.

The ministers have considered the way that some fans attempt to parallel the life of Elvis with the life of Jesus. They see how the stories are similar in many ways, from the humble origins to the betrayal and death. But they point to one crucial difference. The early Christians experienced the power of the Holy Spirit and became followers of Christ long before the Bible was compiled. They would not have known the stories people today are familiar with. Indeed such accounts as the Christmas story would have been totally unknown to most early followers of Christ. They had faith and believed without needing to know the gospel accounts. However, for the followers of Elvis, the process is reversed. It is only when they have heard the stories, and read into them a spiritual significance, that they have started to consider Elvis in a religious light. As Charles Leist puts it:

It is the difference between the story keeping the spirit alive and the spirit keeping the story alive. As long as the story of Elvis is promoted and marketed, as long as people remember, then the spirit of Elvis will continue. With Jesus it is the spirit which keeps the story alive. The story would not live without the gift of the Holy Spirit. That Christ is more than a memory. Christ is a living presence. He is a spirit present with us. And as long as the spirit is with us, the story will continue to live.

*

In a short article in *International Folklore Review*, with the perceptive, but rather long title of "Death, Resurrection and Transfiguration: The Religious Folklore in Elvis Presley Shrines and Souvenirs", Sue Bridwell Beckham quotes a poem she found on a bookmark for sale at a souvenir stall near Elvis Presley's birthplace in Tupelo. Under the title *Abundant Living*, the poem reads,

> Pray: it is the greatest power on earth.
> Love: it is a God-given privilege.
> Read: it is the fountain of wisdom.
> Think: it is the source of power.
> Be friendly: it is the road to happiness.
> Give: it is too short a day to be selfish.
> Play: it is the secret of perpetual youth.
> Laugh: it is the music of the soul.
> Work: it is the price of success.
> Save: it is the secret of security.

The writer then goes on to say that no attribution is provided for the words or the sentiment.

But the implication is clear: true believers will take the message to be Elvis's own whatever the reality of his life. And the structural similarity to the beatitudes from Jesus's "sermon on the mount", no more accurately attributable to Jesus than the Abundant Living creed is to Elvis, leaves no mistake about the implications: this material is scriptural. One can be certain that any of Elvis's followers would be shocked to be accused of confusing Elvis Presley with a Messiah. Such a claim would be considered sacrilege or even blasphemy, but the confusion between the very mortal and corporeal Elvis and the risen saviour of Christianity remains, in the attitudes of his followers, in the powers attributed to Elvis and in the marketing of his memory which the followers easily accept.

Whatever spiritual parallels can be claimed between the lives of Jesus and Elvis, the Elvis theology turns one aspect of Christianity totally on its head. Christians teach that Christ suffered and died on the cross as a selfless act to save others from their sins. It was the ultimate self-sacrifice by God to save and redeem the people he had created in his own image and to whom he had given free will. In the case of Elvis, it is the fans who have endured the suffering for him. Thousands have suffered grief and loss as a result of his death. And whether the death was a fake or brought about by drug abuse, Elvis must carry some of the responsibility for his end. Even the betrayal and "crucifixion" by public exposure has hurt his fans every bit as much as it hurt him. Probably even more so. The fans were also exposed to the possibility of feeling a sense of double betrayal. They shared in Elvis's sense of betrayal by his friends, but also their emotions were exposed to feelings that they too had been badly let down by their hero. Thousands of fans choose to overlook or forgive their hero's weaknesses, but inevitably some considered that even if only a small part of the picture of the drug dependent, incontinent, gun-toting, psychic freak was true, it badly dented their carefully nurtured image of the King.

Doubts and uncertainties have done little to dampen the ardour of most fans. And even those who make no claims to Elvis having any remarkable spiritual purpose still employ religious, and usually Christian, language, to express their feelings. The fans keep writing and pledging their support. New batches of letters arrive at the offices of fan clubs whenever attacks are made on their hero. If the attacks take the form of news allegations about Elvis's private life, letters of solidarity pour in. This one was written by a fan from Lichfield in Staffordshire, reacting to the controversial Albert Goldman dissection of the King's reputation.

> I do not understand why people have the need to write things about Elvis that will ruin his reputation. . . Elvis loved his fans and his music. He was generous, loving and kind. If only his dear mother Gladys had not died. She showed her love to Elvis. No man can ever be perfect. Elvis had his faults. Everybody has faults. Only now Elvis is "away" he cannot stop people like Albert Goldman ruining his reputation.

(Note the interesting use of the word "away", covering the possibility that Elvis might one day make a comeback.)

Many religions in their early days have attracted scorn, ridicule and vilification. The early Christians were mocked and persecuted. The message they preached undermined both the "correct" thinking of the traditional Jews and of the Roman political regime of the day. The Elvis message too is something of a threat, the fans allege, to the liberal establishment mindset of today. The fans' main criticism of Albert Goldman is that he makes Elvis out to be an immature, superficial southern hillbilly. Describing what he sees as its tasteless decor, Goldman says of Graceland that it cost a lot of money to fill up, but nothing in the house is worth a dime. In writing this way, the fans feel, he is sneering at them. They feel he is arrogantly setting himself up as judge of their choices, tastes and values. He exudes a sense of superiority and each barb he aims at Elvis, the fans feel, is also aimed at them.

Yet the fans can claim they have the last laugh. It is to Elvis that ordinary people turn. He is able to give expression to their emotions, he finds the words to speak their thoughts. The middle-class elite cultures of America's east coast and Europe's capitals of learning fail where Elvis succeeds. Elvis can be condemned as lowbrow. His sentiments are coated in sugar. Yet he manages to tap a vein of spirituality in ordinary people which high art and many mainstream churches miss.

It can be said that everyone has a spiritual dimension. Everyone is faced with the ultimate questions at some point. Most people know of love, loneliness, jealousy, patriotism, desolation. But to find expression for these feelings, not many know how to tap the great well of culture and spiritual thought which has accumulated over the centuries. But Elvis, through the electronic means of mass communication now available, makes himself available. Through him they can ponder their loneliness, their weaknesses, their jealousies, their angers, their joys, hopes and celebrations, their powerlessness and then dream the American dream.

Many Elvis fans will not recognize this in themselves, but will admit to Elvis drawing from within them something deeper than ordinary, day-to-day experiences. It is to Elvis's music they turn when needing a quiet moment, to collect thoughts, to grieve, to cry, to remember all the things that might have been, as well as when wanting an excuse for, or an accompaniment to, happier thoughts. Elvis can be associated with love, with relationships and with good times recalled.

How, then, will fans view the idea of being described as members of an Elvis cult? Many will not see it that way. They will be unwilling to label their love for a man and his music as anything resembling a weird sect with occult overtones. It will be irrelevant to them that Elvis filled his mind with numerology and theosophy. To them the Elvis they love is the Elvis they have constructed in their own minds. To them he is the poster on the wall, the intimate sound of his records and a grief at his passing of an intensity seldom experienced. To them Elvis is the spirit alive today in them, his music and his fans. The theology is irrelevant.

But all religions exist at different levels. If the Elvis cult is shaping into a religion, it too will need an underpinning theology. The thinkers will have to be able to show why adoration of Elvis is a valid pursuit. Elvis will have to be shown he was something and somebody special. Was he a Christ or a master, the latest in an ancient line of revelation? Fans talk of his power and his magic and his hold over them.

In time will they not want a philosophical explanation, a coherent body of beliefs which will take the Elvis myth on? If his attraction is just an ephemeral image and a collection of electronic recordings, then is he not destined for the same obscurity as so many other fashions? Elvis fans of the future will need to believe he is more and will indeed live for ever, and that belief requires a theology which can claim an ancient pedigree.

But if that ancient pedigree is the one drawn from Elvis's own interests, it could lead to some very strange beliefs. With a century or two of fermentation, it could take almost any peculiar course. Even today there are hints to be had from the way Elvis fans talk that Elvis is to return to earth, perhaps in some apocalyptic role; a herald perhaps of the end time. If the blueprint for the end contained in the book of Revelation in the Bible, some fans see Elvis as having a part to play. One fan message on the Graceland wall says, "Hoping and praying to see Elvis on a paradise earth one day." And another fan has written, "Elvis, the world needs you."

This is Revelation chapter 20, verses 4 to 6:

I could see the souls of those who had been beheaded for the sake of God's word and their testimony to Jesus, those who had not worshipped the beast and its image or received its mark on forehead or hand. These came to life again and reigned with Christ for a thousand years, though the rest of the dead did not come to life until the thousand years were over. This is the first resurrection. Happy indeed, and one of God's own people, is the man who shares in this first resurrection! Upon such the second death has no claim; but they shall be priests of God and of Christ, and shall reign with him for the thousand years.

Could this be the time of paradise referred to by the writer on the Graceland wall, and Elvis one of the chosen?

Towards the end of the book by Kahlil Gibran, a mystical prose poem called *The Prophet*, which Elvis was fond of reading, is this passage. Fans of Elvis, familiar with the books Elvis read, will no doubt have marked it in their copies, and perhaps imagine Elvis reading aloud:

> Brief were my days among you, and briefer still the words I have spoken.
> But should my voice fade in your ears, and my love vanish in your memory, then I will come again.
> And with a richer heart and lips more yielding to the spirit will I speak.
> Yea, I shall return with the tide,
> And though death may hide me, and the greater silence enfold me, yet again will I seek your understanding.
> And not in vain will I seek.
> If aught I have said is truth, that truth shall reveal itself in a clearer voice, and in words more kin to your thoughts.
> I go with the wind, people of Orphalese, but not down into emptiness;
> And if this day is not a fulfilment of your needs and my love, then let it be a promise till another day.
> Man's needs change, but not his love, nor his desire that his love should satisfy his needs.
> Know, therefore, that from the greater silence I shall return.

A more down to earth approach is taken by George Klein, a friend of Elvis from their school days. He had witnessed Elvis's rise to fame, had been part of that exciting age when rock and roll entered the musical vocabulary of the world. He knew Elvis, the mesmerising performer and the kid who never grew up. He saw the sad final years. His simple epitaph is this: "Think not how Elvis Presley died, but think how Elvis Presley lived."